Mediterranean Diet Cookbook for Beginners

Complete Guide to Mediterranean Lifestyle with Easy, Step-by-Step, and Tasty Recipes You Can Cook At Home Right Now and a 30-Day Kick-Start Meal Plan

Miranda Sharron

Copyright © 2021 - Miranda Sharron

Want to read a FREE sample of this book?
Check this page: https://mirandasharron.aweb.page/p/99408355-5399-461a-b4b2-2549fc7d177f

Enjoy the other books written by Miranda Sharron on Amazon:

Mediterranean Diet Meal Prep Cookbook
https://www.amazon.com/dp/B09NSZ671P

Table of Contents

Introduction — 9

    A Bit of History — 10

    Benefits — 10

    Mediterranean Myths — 11

Chapter 1: The Mediterranean Way — 13

    Freezing Bananas — 13

    Snack Time Favorites — 13

    Jump-Start The Mediterranean Diet Plan — 15

Chapter 2: Mediterranean Breakfast & Brunch Specialties — 16

    Egg Options — 16

        Avocado & Egg Breakfast Sandwich — 16

        Breakfast Couscous — 17

        Brunch Mediterranean Egg Salad — 18

        4-Cheese Zucchini Strata — 19

        Frisco Fried Egg & Cheese Breakfast — 20

        Goat Cheese Frittata & Kale — 21

        Greek Egg Frittata — 22

        Greek Quinoa Breakfast Bowl — 23

        Ham & Egg Cups — 24

        Italian Vegetable Frittata — 25

        Mediterranean Eggs on Toast — 26

        Shakshuka Skillet Dish — 27

        Spinach Omelet — 28

        Turkish Poached Eggs in Garlicky Yogurt Sauce — 29

        Turkish Scrambled Eggs With Tomatoes — 30

    Sweet Breakfast Favorites — 31

        Blackberry-Ginger Overnight Bulgur — 31

Blueberry Muffins 32

Breakfast Quinoa 33

Fig & Ricotta Toast 34

Greek Honey & Walnut Yogurt Bowl 34

Greek Peanut Butter & Banana Yogurt Bowl 35

Honey & Fig Yogurt 35

Mediterranean Eggs on Toast 36

Nutty Banana Oatmeal 37

Pumpkin Pancakes 38

Tahini Date Banana Shake 39

Whole Grain Citrus & Olive Oil Muffins 40

Chapter 3: Mediterranean Salad Specialties 41

Antipasto Salad – Gluten-Free & Keto-Friendly 41

Arugula Salad 42

Avocado Mediterranean Salad 43

Brown Rice Salad 44

Chickpea Salad 45

Fig & Goat Cheese Salad 46

Delightful Quinoa Salad 47

Fruit Salad With Honey-Mint Sauce 48

Greek Tabbouleh Salad 49

Greek Yogurt With Cucumber & Dill Salad 50

Honey-Walnut Salad With Feta & Raisins 51

Lebanese Lentil Salad 52

Sweet & Spicy Jicama Salad 53

Tuna Antipasto Salad 54

Tuna Spinach Salad 55

Watermelon-Olive- Feta & Caper Salad 56

Wrap & Flatbread Options 57

Garden Wrap 57

Kale & Hummus Wrap 58

Mediterranean Flatbread 59

Chapter 4: Mediterranean Soup Specialties 60

Barley-Mushroom Soup 60

Egg & Lemon Greek Soup 61

Homemade Vegetable Soup 62

Lentil Greek Soup 64

Meatball Soup 65

Mediterranean Stew 66

Parmesan Soup - Gluten-Free 67

Persian Chilled Cucumber Soup 68

White Bean Chili – Instant Pot 69

Chapter 5: Mediterranean Seafood Specialties 70

Frozen Italian Fish - Instant Pot 70

Herbed Salmon 71

Moroccan Fish Favorite 72

Pan Seared Mahi-Mahi in Tomato-Mascarpone Sauce 73

Pan-Seared Salmon & Asparagus 74

Pan-Seared Sea Bass 75

Roasted Cod With Olive-Tomato-Caper Tapenade 76

Seared Tuna Steaks 77

Chapter 6: Mediterranean Poultry Specialties 78

Chicken Favorites 78

Baked Popcorn Chicken 78

Braised Chicken With the Trimmings 80

Chicken-Feta Burgers 81

Chicken Gyros With Tzatziki Sauce 82

Chicken Marrakesh 83

Chicken Souvlaki 84

Creamy Tuscan Garlic Chicken - Keto-Adaptable 85

Grape & Grilled Chicken Skewers 86

Lebanese Grilled Shish Tawook – Skewers 87

Lemony Chicken Skewers 88

Lemon-Za'atar -Grilled Chicken 89

Lemon Thyme Chicken With Fingerlings 90

Turkey Favorites 91

Black Olive & Feta Turkey Burgers 91

Turkey Bolognese Sauce 92

Chapter 7: Mediterranean Lean Pork & Lamb Specialties 93

Pork Favorites — 93

- Honey Lemon Pork Chops — 93
- Pork Tenderloin & Couscous - Slow Cooked — 94
- Roasted Balsamic Pork Loin — 95
- Rosemary Pork Loin Chops — 96

Lamb Favorites — 97

- Balsamic Lamb Chops — 97
- Grilled Lamb Chops & Mint — 98
- Grilled Lamb Chops With Tomato-Mint Quinoa — 99
- Lamb Chops With Rosemary & Thyme — 101
- Lamb Lettuce Wraps — 102
- Mediterranean Lamb Bowls — 103
- Mediterranean Lamb Nachos — 104
- Roasted Leg of Lamb With Potatoes — 106

Chapter 8: Mediterranean Lean Beef Specialties — 108

- Beef & Couscous Favorite — 108
- Beef Kofta — 109
- Beef Pitas — 110
- Beef Steaks Crusted in Cumin With Olive-Orange Relish — 111
- Grilled Beef Lettuce Wraps With Garlic-Yogurt Sauce — 112

Chapter 9: Side Dishes & Vegetables — 113

Pasta Dishes — 113

- Broccoli Pasta With White Beans — 113
- Cannellini Pasta — 114
- Linguine & Scallops — 115
- Mediterranean Shrimp Penne — 116
- Rigatoni With Asiago Cheese & Green Olive-Almond Pesto — 117
- Shrimp & Angel Hair Pasta — 118
- Vegetarian Lasagna Roll-Ups — 119

Veggie Options — 121

- Baked Zucchini Sticks — 121
- Chickpea Cauliflower Couscous — 122
- Fasolakia Lathera - Greek Green Beans — 123
- Fried Garlicy Tomatoes — 124

Grilled Zucchini Boats Loaded With Tomatoes & Feta	125
Loaded Portobello Burger	127
Mediterranean Zucchini Casserole	128
Mushroom Kabobs	129
Red Pepper Pasta With Sweet Potatoes	130
Spanakorizo - Greek Spinach & Rice	131
Spinach & Fried Rice With Artichokes & Peppers	132
Stuffed Eggplant	133
Zesty Chargrilled Broccolini	134

Chapter 10: Mediterranean Appetizer & Snack Specialties — **135**

Sweet Snacks — 135

Baked Apricots	135
Blueberry-Coconut Energy Bites	136
Date & Prosciutto Wraps	137
Delicious Energy Bites	137
Easy Roasted Fruit	138
Honey-Almond Peaches	139
Honey Pistachio Roasted Pears	140
Lemon Bars	141
Mediterranean Baked Apples	142
Pasteli - Greek Honey Sesame Bars	143
Poached Cherries	144
Popped Quinoa Crunch Bars	145

Snack Boxes & Trays — 146

All-Green Crudites Basket	146
Charcuterie Bistro Lunch Box	147
Fruit Charcuterie Board	148
Rainbow Heirloom Tomato Bruschetta Tray	149
Tuna Protein Box	150

Other Snacks — 151

Baked Beet Chips	151
Cranberry - Goat Cheese & Walnut Canapés	152
Cucumber Roll-Ups	153
Falafel Smash	154
Grab & Go Snack Jars	155

Mediterranean Eggplant Chips	156
Pita Pizzas & Hummus	157
Smoked Salmon & Avocado Summer Rolls	158

Dips — 159

Feta Dip	159
Healthy Basil Pesto	160
Spring Pea & Fava Bean Guacamole With Root Chips	161

Chapter 11: Mediterranean Dessert Specialties — 163

Fanouropita - Saint Fanourios Cake	163
Greek Yogurt Cheesecake	164
Greek Yogurt Parfait With Nuts & Kahlua	165
Greek Yogurt Pumpkin Parfait	166
Honey Pie With Ricotta Cheese	167
Italian Apple & Olive Oil Cake	168
Mango-Peach & Nectarine & Crumble	169
Mediterranean Chocolate Cake	170
Middle Eastern Rice Pudding	171
Raspberry Clafoutis	172
Sweet Ricotta & Strawberry Parfaits	173
Tahini Brownies	174

Chapter 12: Mediterranean 30-Day Kick-Start Meal Plan — 175

Week One Kick-Off	175
Week Two Mediterranean Plan	177
Week Three Mediterranean Plan	178
Week Four Mediterranean Plan	179
Week Five Mediterranean Plan	180

Introduction

Congratulations on your purchase of the *Mediterranean Diet Cookbook for Beginners,* and thank you for doing so. The following chapters will discuss the Mediterranean way of dining basics by using a diet plan used in countries such as Spain, Greece, and other Mediterranean locations dating back to the 1960s. It was discovered when researchers noticed these individuals were much healthier when compared to the Americans and also had such a low risk of so many diseases that could be deadly.

You can lose and maintain a healthy weight and discover a sustainable way to reduce any disease-causing inflammation. The fortunate part of the diet plan (also called the Med Diet) is there's no need to journey to an exotic country to enjoy the cuisine. Merely prepare the delicious meals using items in your cupboards and refrigerator using your oven and stovetop.

You will also discover that you will have more energy while on the Mediterranean diet plan, and with that energy, you can become more active. Motivation will be the leader you head toward your new lifestyle making crucial changes along the road to success.

The Mediterranean eating style gives you a huge advantage since you do *not* need to track any points or weigh out any portions for each of your meals. You will quickly learn how easy the plan is and know you can realistically stick to it.

Once you get the methods figured out, you will love the many different spices and herbs that can liven up a normally drab meal. You will quickly discover which ones are your favorite foods. There are several items listed that will provide you with an idea of how delicious the food is.

The World Health Organization (WHO) recommends you consume a minimum of eight to eleven cups of water each day if you are a woman, ten to fifteen if you are a man. WHO revealed millions of deaths annually are attributed to too little vegetable and fruit intake. Therefore, they also support the basis of the Mediterranean plan.

A Bit of History

Ancel Keys, a scientist, and his colleagues (included Paul Dudley which later became President Eisenhower's cardiac physician, conducted a *Seven Countries Study* in the years following World War II) comparing individuals in the United States to those living in Crete, a Mediterranean island. He examined the plan, testing individuals of all ages using the 'so-called' Mediterranean Diet.

The long-running study examined 13,000 middle-aged men (remember the times) in the Netherlands, Yugoslavia (at that time), the United States, Finland, Greece, Italy, and Japan. It became evident the fish, vegetables, fruits, beans, and grains were the healthiest meals possible, even after the deprivations of WWII. This was the starting point!

Benefits

Let's consider the benefits provided using the Mediterranean techniques:

- Lose Weight in a Healthy Way
- A Diet Low in Sugar and Processed Foods
- Alzheimer's Risk factors are Reduced
- Lowered Risk of Heart Disease and Strokes
- Parkinson's Risk Factors are Reduced
- Asthma Symptoms are reduced
- Diabetes Prevention and Treatment
- Expanded lifespan with the Mediterranean method
- Metabolic Complications of Obesity reduced with the plan
- You relax more and remove excess stressing following the plan.
- Your vision should improve.
- Improved agility with the Mediterranean plan.

Mediterranean Myths

#1: The Myth: Eat lots of bread and big pasta dishes; it's a Mediterranean lifestyle!
The Fact: Customarily, the diet uses pasta as a side dish with about a half to a one-cup serving. The remainder of the meal involves fish, or a small serving of grass-fed or organic, meat, veggies, healthy salads, and possibly a piece of sliced bread.

#2: The Myth: If I have one glass of wine, three is much better.
The Fact: The Mediterranean cuisine ideally consumes moderate red wine; for men at two, and women only one drink daily. Wine does have health benefits, but too many can be hazardous to your heart.

#3: The Myth: It's more expensive to eat using a Mediterranean diet.
The Fact: The Med diet will create meals using lentils and beans for a protein source (whole grains and plants). These are much less expensive than processed/packaged food.

#4: The Myth: Everyone living in the Mediterranean areas are healthy.
The Fact: Unfortunately, not all regions or countries practice the same healthy eating habits. For example, many in the northern segment of Italy use lard for their cooking needs, which lean towards more saturated fats. Those in the southern areas primarily use olive oil.

#5: The Myth: Mediterranean cuisine allows me to eat as much cheese as I desire.
The Fact: Consuming too much cheese can quickly add up too many unwanted saturated fats and calories. Cheese should be consumed moderately using strongly flavored cheese such as goat or feta cheese. You want the flavor, not the added 'bad' fats.

#6: The Myth: The Med diet plan is just about the food.
The Fact: As you will discover, food is an essential part of the plan, but lifestyle changes are also part of the Mediterranean way. Enjoying a healthy plan is just as important as the food on your plate. You want to enjoy life and all it offers.

#7: The Myth: It is difficult to follow the Mediterranean diet plan.
The Fact: Difficult is a bad choice of words when comparing the Med plan with other diets. You're merely attempting to raise the intake of a variety of food items while decreasing the use in others. It is no different than changing any other 'behavioral' pattern.

#8: The Myth: You cannot prepare 'cooked' foods using extra-virgin (EVOO) olive oil.

The Fact: Extra-virgin oil will lose part of its exclusive flavor during cooking, but it doesn't become unhealthful. However, it does maintain a lower "smoke point" (the point when an oil starts to smoke and break down) than refined oils like canola oil; it's high enough to be an excellent option for almost all cooking at home.

#9: The Myth: I can be like the Mediterranean 'lifers' and eat huge meals without gaining weight!

The Fact: The Med diet plan allows you to enjoy portions of low-calorie food items versus the over-rated high-calorie foods. The palette consists of raw and cooked veggies, lean meat portions, legumes, and grains *versus* the US way of eating with its abundant orders of burgers and fries. You get the point!

#10: The Myth: You can forget going to the gym!

The Fact: This one causes many issues and is technically a true statement (with a few flaws). You do not necessarily need to go to the gym to model your life to the Mediterranean way of living. Fifty to sixty years ago, they were performing manual work and remained active. Today, individuals tend to be a bit lazy, so you need to do a few exercises to stay in shape.

Let's go with another step!

Chapter 1: The Mediterranean Way

The Mediterranean diet plan is heart-healthy, emphasizing the plant-based eating approach. It is loaded with healthy fats, fruits, and veggies, including omega-3 fatty acids from fish and olive oil. This diet is also rich in whole grains, nuts, and legumes.

You will be limiting or avoiding sugary foods, red meat, and dairy. However, in small portions, cheese and yogurt are acceptable. Consider you are filling your plate with foods from the colors of the rainbow.

You are also able to enjoy red wine in moderate amounts while using the Mediterranean diet. For women, you are allowed five ounces daily, whereas men are allowed ten ounces per day. A healthier lifestyle does not mean you have to eliminate your social life. Merely remember to indulge using moderation.

The Mediterranean way of eating is typically rich in healthy plant foods and lower in animal foods. It places more of a focus on fish and seafood. It is predominantly beneficial because you will not be hungry!

The Mediterranean techniques emphasize getting plenty of exercise and primarily consuming whole grains, fruits, legumes, vegetables, and nuts.

It would be best if you consider replacing butter with healthy fats, including canola or olive oil. Instead of salt, use spices and different herbs. Stick by the Mediterranean pyramid of foods, and you won't go wrong!

Freezing Bananas

You will discover a way to use bananas anytime you desire. The best way to prepare the bananas is to peel and slice them into one to two-inch pieces. Prep a baking tray with a sheet of waxed paper or parchment paper. Arrange the banana slices on the tray and freeze them for an hour or two hours. Once frozen, store them in a bag or plastic container for another time.

Snack Time Favorites

The best path to weight loss is by making healthy food choices. So, try some of these foods at those times when you do not have the time for a meal:

Apple Slices & Almond Butter: Enjoy a quick snack by removing the apple cores (with or without the peel) and add your favorite almond butter. Quench your sweet tooth before it's time for your next meal.

Greek Yogurt & Fruit: Enjoy a protein-rich snack of some Greek yogurt. Garnish the yogurt with some sunflower seeds, a few delicious berries, and a honey drizzle for a tasty mid-afternoon snack.

Dates & Figs: These are some products that grow well in the Mediterranean climate. They are also a sweet treat when you are too busy to prepare a snack.

Pita & Hummus: You can have some sesame paste (tahini) and chickpeas in the form of hummus. Consider making some at home, but you can also purchase it ready-made. Make sure you read the label and choose one with a limited amount of preservatives. You can select a whole-wheat piece of pita bread with a hummus spread for a delicious snack.

Hummus-Stuffed Peppers: Grab your favorite baby bell peppers and add the filling of choice for a quick pick-me-up snack anytime!

Kalamata Olives: When you are in a rush, nothing says it all like a handful of healthy olives. They are rich in many antioxidants, including oleic acid. Mix them up with a small amount of feta cheese for an additional boost.

Sun-Dried Tomato & Goat Cheese Spread: The rich flavor of the sun-dried tomatoes is only the beginning since it is full of calcium, iron, vitamin C, vitamin A, and lycopene. It also provides a heart-healthy boost since it is often packed in olive oil.

Chickpea Salad in a Jiffy: Toss together some fresh tomatoes, olives, cucumbers, and chickpeas. Toss with a tangy lemon dressing and fresh herbs.

Prepare a Meze: If you like to open the fridge in search of something good, why not have a dishful of various foods? Make a basic container of carrot sticks, tomatoes, olives, cucumber, and cheese.

Make it a point to have healthier options when you have an urge for a loaded calorie dish!

Jump-Start The Mediterranean Diet Plan

Begin with small steps as you begin changing your eating habits using a Mediterranean cuisine diet plan. Try these ways.

- Omit butter and use olive oil (extra-virgin) to sauté your food.

- Add more veggies and fruits with a healthy salad as a side dish or other veggies. Snack on fruit instead of chips.

- Eliminate refined rice, pasta, and bread by opting for whole grains.

- Try to reduce your intake of red meat. Instead, enjoy fish at least twice per week.

Are you enjoying this book? If so, I would be very grateful if you could leave a short review on Amazon. It's very important to me! Thank you!

Chapter 2: Mediterranean Breakfast & Brunch Specialties

Egg Options

Avocado & Egg Breakfast Sandwich

Servings Provided: 2

Preparation & Cooking Time: 10-15 minutes

What You Need
- Toasted bread slices - whole wheat (4)
- Pitted avocado (1)
- Steamed asparagus spears (8-12)
- Sliced - hard-boiled egg (1)
- Olive oil (as needed)
- Freshly ground pepper & coarse sea salt (as desired)
- Optional: Dijon mustard

How To Prepare
1. Peel and mash the avocado. Toast the bread.
2. Prepare the sandwich by applying mustard with a layer of avocado.
3. Add the asparagus spears and eggs.
4. Now, please give it a spritz of oil with a bit of pepper and salt. Close and serve.

Breakfast Couscous

Servings Provided: 4-6 or 3 cups cooked

Preparation & Cooking Time: 25 minutes

What You Need

- Uncooked whole-wheat couscous (1 cup)
- Low-fat 1% milk (3 cups)
- Dried currants (.5 cup)
- Cinnamon stick (2-inch stick)
- Dried apricots (.5 cup)
- Salt (.25 tsp.)
- Dark brown sugar - divided (6 tsp.)
- Melted butter - divided (4 tsp.)

How To Prepare

1. Using the med-hi setting on the stovetop, place a large saucepan and add the cinnamon stick and milk. Heat it until you see bubble formations along the edges. (Do not boil.)
2. Remove from the burner and blend in the apricots, couscous, salt, currants, and four teaspoons of brown sugar. Place a lid on the pan and set aside (15 min.).
3. Now, take the top off and throw away the cinnamon stick.
4. Serve and garnish with ½ teaspoon of brown sugar and a teaspoon of melted butter. This dish can be used for dinner with a bit of a twist, but this one has dried fruit and brown sugar, which is ideal for breakfast!

Brunch Mediterranean Egg Salad

Servings Provided: 4

Preparation & Cooking Time: 5-10 minutes

What You Need

- Hard-boiled eggs (8 large)
- Chopped cucumber (.5 cup)
- Red onion (.5 cup)
- Sun-dried tomatoes (.5 cup)
- Olives (.25 cup)
- Lemon juice (1 splash)
- Plain Greek yogurt (.5 cup)
- Cumin (.25 tsp.)
- Oregano (1.5 tsp.)
- Black pepper (as desired)
- Sea salt (.5 tsp.)

How To Prepare

1. Drain off the excess oil from the tomatoes. Then, chop the veggies and eggs.
2. Toss the eggs with the onion, tomatoes, olives, and cucumber.
3. Now, mix in the spices, yogurt, and lemon juice.
4. Enjoy it for about seven days when kept in the refrigerator.

4-Cheese Zucchini Strata

Servings Provided: 8

Preparation & Cooking Time: Varies – 3 hours

What You Need

- Yellow summer squash/zucchini (4 medium/5 cups)
- Olive oil (2 tbsp.)
- Bite-sized Italian flatbread - ex. - Italian focaccia (8 cups)
- Shredded Provolone & white cheddar cheese (4 oz./1 cup each)
- Grated parmesan (.5 cup)
- Crumbled feta (2 oz./56 g)
- Milk (2 cups)
- Eggs (7 slightly beaten)
- Freshly snipped parsley (2 tbsp.)
- Salt & black pepper (.5 tsp. each)
- Also Needed: 3-qt./2.8 l. - rectangular/oval baking dish +Extra-large skillet

How To Prepare

1. Slice the zucchini into halves and cut them into ¼-inch pieces. Prepare the squash in the skillet (med-high) using hot oil. Stir occasionally - until browned.
2. Lightly grease the baking dish and place ½ of the bread pieces in the bottom. Top it off with half of the squash along with each of the cheeses. Repeat with layers.
3. Mix the milk, eggs, pepper, and salt in a large mixing container. Empty it evenly over the layers and gently press it over the surface.
4. Cover with some plastic wrap and chill (2-24 hr.).
5. When ready to prepare, set the oven to 325° Fahrenheit/163° Celsius.
6. Bake 45-50 minutes. It should be set. Let it rest about ten minutes before serving. Now, please give it a sprinkle of parsley to serve.

Frisco Fried Egg & Cheese Breakfast

Servings Provided: 4

Preparation & Cooking Time: 10 minutes

What You Need

- Shredded parmesan cheese (.5 cup or 2 oz./56 g)
- Eggs (4)
- Provolone cheese (4 slices)
- Black pepper & salt (to your liking)
- Split-toasted English muffins (4)
- Dried tomatoes in olive oil (.25 cup - thinly sliced)
- Baby arugula (1 cup)
- Also Needed: Nonstick skillet or 12-inch/30-cm griddle

How To Prepare

1. Heat the skillet using the low-temperature setting.
2. Sprinkle the cheese into (4) four-inch rounds on the skillet and cook for one minute.
3. Crack the eggs over the cheese with a sprinkle of pepper and salt. Fry them till the yolks are as desired (4-5 min.).
4. Top the sandwich with the provolone and prepare it until it's melted.
5. Layer the muffin bottoms with the tomatoes.
6. Next, add the eggs, arugula, and tops of the muffin to serve.

Goat Cheese Frittata & Kale

Servings Provided: 6

Preparation & Cooking Time: 20 minutes

What You Need

- Medium onion (1)
- Fresh kale (2 cups - torn)
- Olive oil (2 tsp.)
- Eggs (6)
- Egg whites (4)
- Black pepper (.125 tsp.)
- Salt (.25 tsp.)
- Dried tomatoes (.25 cup)
- Goat cheese (1 oz./28 g)

How To Prepare

1. Thinly slice the onion in half. Drain and thinly slice the tomatoes and crumble the cheese.
2. Place the oven rack four inches from the heating element.
3. Heat the oven broiler while cooking the kale and onion using the medium temperature setting (10 min.)
4. Whisk the eggs with pepper and salt. Pour the mix into the skillet using the med-low heat setting.
5. When the edges are almost set, sprinkle them with tomatoes and cheese.
6. Transfer them to the broiler for one to two minutes.
7. Slice them into six wedges to serve.

Greek Egg Frittata

Servings Provided: 6

Preparation & Cooking Time: 25 minutes

What You Need

- Eggs (6)
- Cream/milk (.5 cup)
- Diced tomatoes (.5 cup)
- Spanish olives (.25 cup)
- Kalamata olives (.25 cup)
- Spinach (1 cup)
- Salt (1 tsp.)
- Feta (.25 cup)
- Pepper (.5 tsp.)
- Oregano (1 tsp.)
- Also Needed: Quiche pan or 8-inch/20-cm pie pan

How To Prepare

1. Warm the oven to 400° Fahrenheit/204° Celsius. Grease the baking pan.
2. Dice the tomatoes and chop the spinach. Crumble the feta.
3. Whisk the milk and eggs with the remainder of the fixings.
4. Bake until the eggs are set (15-20 min.).

Greek Quinoa Breakfast Bowl

Servings Provided: 12

Preparation & Cooking Time: 20 minutes

What You Need

- Olive oil (1 tsp.)
- Eggs (12)
- Garlic (1 tsp. - granulated)
- Black pepper and salt (.5 tsp. each)
- Onion powder (1 tsp.)
- Greek yogurt - plain (.25 cup)
- Baby spinach (1 oz./28 g)
- Cherry tomatoes (1-pint)
- Feta cheese (1 cup)
- Quinoa (2 cups - cooked)

How To Prepare

1. Whisk the yogurt, eggs, garlic, pepper, salt, onion powder in a mixing container.
2. Warm oil in a big skillet - toss in the spinach to sauté till it's wilted (3-4 min.).
3. Slice the tomatoes into halves and add to the mixture – continue to sauté (another 3-4 min.).
4. Fold in the egg mixture (step 1) and cook (7-9 min.).
5. When set, blend in the feta and quinoa. Simmer until hot and serve.

Ham & Egg Cups

Servings Provided: 8

Preparation & Cooking Time: 30-35 minutes

What You Need

- Deli cooked ham (8 thin slices)
- Mozzarella cheese (.25 cup or 1 oz.)
- Eggs (8)
- Optional: Basil (8 tsp.)
- Black pepper
- Cherry/grape tomatoes (8)
- Also Needed:
- Muffin tin (8 count)
- Non-stick cooking spray

How To Prepare

1. Set the oven temperature at 350° Fahrenheit/177° Celsius. Coat the muffin tin cups with the spray.
2. Press the ham slice into the bottom and add the cheese to each of the prepared cups.
3. Break an egg into the cup and sprinkle with pepper. Add the pesto, if using. Slice the tomatoes into halves and place them on each of the cups.
4. Bake 18 to 20 minutes. The egg whites should be set, similar to a regular poached egg. Leave them in the cups for three to five minutes. Then, carefully take the cups out of the tin and serve.

Italian Vegetable Frittata

Servings Provided: 8

Preparation & Cooking Time: 45 minutes

What You Need

- Bell pepper (1 small red)
- Green onions (2)
- Zucchini (1 small)
- Broccoli cut into small florets (4 oz. or 110 g)
- Black pepper & Kosher salt (a big pinch of each)
- Olive oil (3 tbsp.)
- Eggs (7 large)
- Optional: Baking powder (.25 tsp.)
- Whole milk (.25 cup)
- Crumbled feta cheese (.33 + more to serve)
- Fresh thyme (1 tsp.)
- Fresh parsley (.33 + more to serve)
- Also Needed: 10-inch cast-iron or oven-safe pan

How To Prepare

1. Warm the oven to 450° Fahrenheit/232° Celsius and position a rack in the middle. Put a rimmed pan/sheet in the oven to heat.
2. Chop the broccoli into florets. Core and chop the bell pepper and dice the zucchini into small pieces. Roughly chop the green onions (green + white pieces).
3. Toss the bell peppers, zucchini, green onion, broccoli, pepper, and salt into a mixing container. Spritz with a little oil (2-3 tbsp.) and toss to ensure all the veggies are well-coated in the oil.
4. Carefully transfer the pan from the oven using oven mitts. Spread the veggies on the heated pan, place them back into the oven, and cook until the veggies are soft and somewhat charred (15 min.).
5. Lower the temperature setting to 400° Fahrenheit/204° Celsius.
6. Whisk the eggs with the baking powder, milk, feta, parsley, thyme, pepper, and salt. Fold in the roasted vegetables.

7. Prepare the skillet (bottom & sides) using a med-high temperature setting. Pour in the oil, heating till it shimmers. Scoop the egg and veggie mixture into the pan to cook until the bottom of the eggs settles (2-3 min.).
8. Put the pan to the heated oven to cook until the center of the eggs is thoroughly cooked, and the center of the frittata is firm and no longer runny (8-10 min.).
9. Serve with more feta cheese and a garnish of fresh parsley.

Mediterranean Eggs on Toast

Servings Provided: 2

Preparation & Cooking Time: 10-15 minutes

What You'll Need:
- Milk (2 tbsp.)
- Eggs (4)
- Olive oil (1 tbsp.)
- Whole wheat bread (2 slices)
- Black pitted olives (6)
- Sliced chorizo sausage (2 oz. or 56 g)
- Onion (1)

How To Prepare
1. Whip/whisk the milk and eggs in a medium container and set them to the side. Using medium heat, pour the oil into a skillet. Thinly slice and sauté the onion (4 min.).
2. Combine the sausage and continue cooking until crispy, approximately two to three minutes. Toss in the olives and stir in the eggs.
3. Cook for two minutes for a soft scrambled egg. Toast the bread and add the egg on top with chives and pepper.

Shakshuka Skillet Dish

Servings Provided: 6

Preparation & Cooking Time: 40 minutes

What You Need

- Sweet pepper (1 large)
- Onion (1 large)
- Garlic (3 cloves)
- Jalapeno chili pepper (1)
- Olive oil (2 tbsp.)
- Kosher salt (.5 tsp.)
- Ground cumin & turmeric (1 tsp. each)
- Black pepper (.25 tsp.)
- Sweet paprika (1 tsp.)
- Whole plum tomatoes with juices (28 oz./790 g can)
- Eggs (6)
- Feta cheese
- For the Garnish: Oregano & fresh cilantro

How To Prepare

1. Chop the peppers, onion, and jalapeno (seeds removed). Coarsely chop the tomatoes.
2. Warm oil in a big skillet using a medium-temperature setting. Toss in the peppers, onion, jalapeno, garlic, paprika, cumin, pepper, salt, and turmeric.
3. Cook about ten minutes. Stir in the tomatoes with liquids. Once it starts to boil; reduce the heat and continue cooking slowly ten minutes. Stir occasionally.
4. Add one egg at a time into a bowl and gently add over the sauce. Cover and lower the heat. Cook about five to ten minutes.

Spinach Omelet

Servings Provided: 4

Preparation & Cooking Time: 30 minutes

What You Need
- Large tomatoes (4)
- Flat-leaf parsley (1 tbsp.)
- Onion (1 small)
- Garlic clove (1 clove)
- Olive oil (3 tbsp.)
- Eggs (8)
- Black pepper (.25 tsp.)
- Fine-grain sea salt (1 tsp.)
- Feta cheese (2 oz./56 g)

How To Prepare
1. Remove the core and chop the tomatoes, onion, and parsley.
2. Warm the oven to reach 400° Fahrenheit/204° Celsius.
3. Add the oil into a cast-iron skillet using a high-temperature setting. Toss in the onions and sauté them until softened (5-7 min.).
4. Pour in the garlic, tomatoes, pepper, and salt.
5. Sauté for about five minutes and add the whisked eggs. Stir and cook for three to five minutes. When the bottom is set, put the skillet into the hot oven. Continue cooking for another; five minutes.
6. Transfer to the countertop and top it off with the parsley and feta. Serve warm.

Turkish Poached Eggs in Garlicky Yogurt Sauce

Servings Provided: 2

Preparation & Cooking Time: 20 minutes

What You Need

- Plain Greek yogurt - whole milk - room temperature (1 cup)
- Garlic cloves (1 to 2)
- Eggs (2)
- Kosher salt (1 dash)
- Olive oil (3 tbsp.)
- Optional: Vinegar (1-2 tbsp.)
- Aleppo pepper/red pepper flakes (2 tsp.)

How To Prepare

1. Whisk the room-temp yogurt and finely minced garlic with salt. Scoop the yogurt mixture into serving dishes and set aside.
2. Prepare a pot of water to boiling with the vinegar.
3. Meanwhile, break an egg into a small fine-mesh sieve over a small mixing container. Gently swirl the eggs in the sieve to drain the liquid part of the egg whites. Transfer the egg to a ramekin.
4. When the water is ready, stir the water to create a vortex. Quickly add the egg to the middle of the vortex and cook (2-3 min.).
5. When ready, scoop the egg onto a plate lined with parchment paper.
6. Prepare and cook the second egg exactly as you did the first.
7. Now, prepare the olive oil sauce by warming the oil and Aleppo pepper (medium temp). Quickly transfer the poached eggs to the prepared yogurt bowls with a drizzle with the heated oil.
8. Serve with your favorite rustic bread.

Turkish Scrambled Eggs With Tomatoes

Servings Provided: 4

Preparation & Cooking Time: 25 minutes

What You'll Need:
- Olive oil (2 tbsp.)
- Yellow onion (1 medium)
- Green bell pepper - Anaheim or Holland peppers ok also (1)
- Kosher salt
- Vine-ripe tomatoes (2)
- Tomato paste (3 tbsp.)
- Black pepper
- Dried oregano (.5 tsp.)
- Aleppo pepper (1 tsp. + as desired)
- Large eggs (4 beaten)
- Optional for Spicer Dish: Crushed red pepper flakes
- Optional to Serve: French baguette (1)
- Suggested: 10-inch/25-cm skillet

How To Prepare
1. Core chop and seed the peppers and chop the onion.
2. Warm two tablespoons of oil in a skillet using a medium-temperature setting.
3. Toss in the onions and peppers with a shake of salt. Sauté them stirring often till they're softer - not browned (4 to 5 min.).
4. Mix in the tomatoes and tomato paste with a tiny bit more salt, black pepper, oregano, and Aleppo pepper. Sauté for a few minutes till the tomatoes soften, but still hold their shape (5-7 min.).
5. Push the tomato and pepper mixture to one side of the pan. Adjust the temperature setting to medium-low. Whisk and add the egg, cook briefly, stirring gently as needed until the eggs are just set.
6. Now, fold the tomato mixture into the eggs.
7. Finish with a little EVOO and pepper flakes for an extra kick.
8. Serve promptly with thick slices of bread.

Sweet Breakfast Favorites

Blackberry-Ginger Overnight Bulgur

Servings Provided: 2

Preparation & Cooking Time: varies to overnight

What You Need
- Whole-milk Greek yogurt – plain (.66 or 2/3 cup)
- Refrigerated coconut milk (3 tbsp.)
- Bulgur (.25 cup)
- Honey (2 tbsp.)
- Snipped crystallized ginger (1 tbsp.) or ground (.25 tsp.)
- Blackberries (.25 cup)

How To Prepare
1. Combine the fixings, omitting the berries in two ½-pint jars. Top with the berries.
2. Place a lid on the jar and pop it in the fridge overnight or up to three days.
3. Stir thoroughly before serving.

Blueberry Muffins

Servings Provided: 24

Preparation & Cooking Time: 28-30 minutes

What You Need

Dry Fixings:

- Whole wheat flour & all-purpose (2 cups each)
- Sugar (.66 or 2/3 cup)
- Baking powder (6 tsp.)
- Salt (1 tsp.)
- Blueberries - defrost if frozen (2 cups)

Wet Fixings:

- Eggs (2)
- Olive oil (2/3 cup)
- Milk - your choice (2 cups)

How To Prepare

1. Set the oven to reach 400° Fahrenheit/204° Celsius. Spritz the baking tin with a spritz of oil or use paper holders.
2. Measure and add the dry components in a mixing container.
3. Gently, stir in blueberries.
4. Combine the wet ones with the dry ingredients – combining well to make the batter.
5. Add the mix to the prepared cups.
6. Bake until a knife inserted in its center comes out clean (18 min.).

Breakfast Quinoa

Servings Provided: 4

Preparation & Cooking Time: 25 minutes

What You Need

- Raw almonds (.25 cup)
- Cinnamon (1 tsp.)
- Quinoa (1 cup)
- Milk (2 cups)
- Sea salt (1 tsp.)
- Honey (2 tbsp.)
- Vanilla extract (1 tsp.)
- Dried pitted dates (2)
- Dried apricots (5)

How To Prepare

1. Toast the almonds in a skillet using the medium-temperature setting until just golden (3-5 min.) and set aside.
2. Finely chop the apricots, and dates, and almonds.
3. Prepare a saucepan set on the medium-temperature setting to warm the quinoa and cinnamon. Pour in the milk and salt. Wait for it to boil and lower the temperature setting to low. Put a lid on the bot to simmer for 15 minutes.
4. When ready, mix in the dates, apricots, honey, and vanilla. Stir and serve with the rest of the almonds.

Fig & Ricotta Toast

Servings Provided: 1

Preparation & Cooking Time: 5 minutes

What You Need

- Crusty whole-grain bread (1 slice @ .5-inch-thick)
- Part-skim ricotta cheese (.25 cup)
- Fresh fig - sliced (1) or dried (2)
- Toasted almonds (1 tsp. - sliced)
- Honey (1 tsp.)
- Flaky sea salt (1 pinch)

How To Prepare

1. Prepare the toast as desired.
2. Top it off with the cheese, figs.
3. Give it a spritz of honey and salt to serve.

Greek Honey & Walnut Yogurt Bowl

Servings Provided: 1

Preparation & Cooking Time: 7-8 minutes

What You Need

- Greek yogurt - 0% fat (.75 cup)
- Walnuts (4 halves)
- Cinnamon (.25 tsp.)
- Honey (1 tsp.)

How To Prepare

1. Toss each of the fixings in a serving dish and serve.

Greek Peanut Butter & Banana Yogurt Bowl

Servings Provided: 4

Preparation & Cooking Time: 5 minutes

What You Need
- Medium bananas (2)
- Flaxseed meal (.25 cup)
- Nutmeg (1 tsp.)
- Peanut butter (.25 cup)
- Greek yogurt - vanilla (4 cups)

How To Prepare
1. Peel and slice the bananas. Portion the yogurt into serving dishes. Top each one with sliced bananas.
2. Microwave the peanut butter for 30 to 40 seconds until thoroughly melted.
3. Drizzle the peanut butter over the banana slices and dust using a bit of flaxseed meal.
4. Garnish using the nutmeg and serve.

Honey & Fig Yogurt

Servings Provided: 1

Preparation & Cooking Time: 3-4 minutes

What You'll Need:
- Sliced dried figs (3)
- Plain yogurt – low-fat (.66 or 2/3 cup)
- Honey (2 tsp.)

How To Prepare
1. Toss the ingredients into a bowl.
2. Stir and serve.

Mediterranean Eggs on Toast

Servings Provided: 2

Preparation & Cooking Time: 15 minutes

What You Need

- Milk (2 tbsp.)
- Eggs (4)
- Olive oil (1 tbsp.)
- Bread - whole wheat (2 slices)
- Black pitted olives (6)
- Chorizo sausage (2 oz./56 g sliced)
- Onion (1)

How To Prepare

1. Whip/whisk the milk and eggs in a medium container and set them to the side. Using medium heat, pour the oil into a skillet. Thinly slice and sauté the onion for four minutes.
2. Combine the sausage and continue cooking until crispy, approximately two to three minutes. Toss in the olives and stir in the eggs.
3. Cook for two minutes for a soft scrambled egg. Toast the bread and add the egg on top with chives and pepper.

Nutty Banana Oatmeal

Servings Provided: 1

Preparation & Cooking Time: 5-6 minutes

What You Need

- Walnuts (2 tbsp.)
- Quick-cooking oats (.25 cup)
- Flax seeds (1 tsp.)
- Honey (3 tbsp.)
- Skim milk (.5 cup)
- Banana (1)

How To Prepare

1. Chop the walnuts and peel the banana. Mix all of the fixings in a microwaveable-safe dish, except for the banana.
2. Cook two minutes on high in the microwave. Use a fork to mash and stir in the banana. Serve hot!

Pumpkin Pancakes

Servings Provided: 6

Preparation & Cooking Time: 15 minutes

What You Need

- Vinegar (2 tbsp.)
- Milk (1.5 cups)
- Egg (1)
- Vegetable oil (2 tbsp.)
- Pumpkin puree (1 cup)
- Baking soda (1 tsp.)
- A-P flour (2 cups)
- Allspice - ground (1 tsp.)
- Brown sugar (3 tbsp.)
- Salt (.5 tsp.)
- Baking powder (2 tsp.)
- Ginger - ground (.5 tsp.)
- Cinnamon (1 tsp.)

How To Prepare

1. Whisk the vinegar, oil, egg, pumpkin, and milk.
2. Combine the salt, ginger, cinnamon, allspice, baking soda, brown sugar, flour, and baking powder in a separate container.
3. Stir the fixings together.
4. Warm a skillet on the stovetop (med-high heat).
5. Dump the batter into the griddle and brown on both sides.

Tahini Date Banana Shake

Servings Provided: 3 cups

Preparation & Cooking Time: 5 minutes

What You Need
- Frozen bananas (2)
- Medjool dates (4)
- Tahini (.25 cup)
- Ice (.25 cup)
- Almond milk - unsweetened (1.5 cups)
- Ground cinnamon (a pinch/as desired)

How To Prepare
1. Slice the bananas and pit the dates. Crush the ice if desired before adding it to the blender.
2. Add the bananas first with the rest of the fixings into the blender.
3. Pulse until your shake is thickened and silky.
4. Serve them with a garnish of ground cinnamon.

Whole Grain Citrus & Olive Oil Muffins

Servings Provided: 12

Preparation & Cooking Time: 32-35 minutes

What You Need

- Spelt flour (1.5 cups)
- Rolled oats (.25 cup)
- Baking powder (2.5 tsp.)
- Sea salt (.5 tsp.)
- Cinnamon (.5 tsp.)
- Egg (1)
- Olive oil (.33 cup)
- Oranges - juiced (1-2 medium or .33 cup)
- Almond milk - unsweetened (.33 or 1/3 cup)
- Maple syrup (.33 cup)
- Vanilla powder/extract (.5 tsp.)
- Orange - zested (1 medium or .5 tbsp.)
- Carrot (1 grated)
- Optional: Chopped almonds (.25 cup)

How To Prepare

1. Warm the oven to 375° Fahrenheit/191° Celsius. Prepare a muffin pan with paper liners.
2. Whisk the flour with the rolled oats, salt, baking powder, and cinnamon in a mixing container.
3. Use another dish to whisk the egg with the orange juice, oil, almond milk, vanilla, maple syrup, and orange zest. Mix with the dry fixings till incorporated. Lightly mix in the grated carrot.
4. Pour the batter into the muffin tins (3/4 full) and add the chopped almonds.
5. Bake until done or spring back when gently pushed in the center (16-19 min.).
6. Let them cool for about five minutes, then transfer them onto a wire rack to thoroughly cooled before serving or storing.

Chapter 3: Mediterranean Salad Specialties

Antipasto Salad — Gluten-Free & Keto-Friendly

Servings Provided: 3

Preparation & Cooking Time: 10 minutes

What You Need

- Hearts romaine (1 large head or 2 medium)
- Artichoke hearts (.5 cup)
- Salami or pepperoni (4 oz./110 g)
- Prosciutto (4 oz.)
- Olives - black & green mixed (.5 cup)
- Hot/sweet peppers - pickled or roasted (.5 cup)
- Italian dressing (as desired)

How To Prepare

1. Chop the romaine and slice the artichokes. Slice the prosciutto into strips and cube the salami.
2. Toss each of the fixings in an oversized salad dish/bowl.
3. Toss with dressing to serve.
4. You will have 462 calories with 41 g of fat but only two grams of net carbs.

Arugula Salad

Servings Provided: 4

Preparation & Cooking Time: 6-10 minutes

What You Need

- Arugula leaves (4 cups)
- Grated parmesan cheese (.25 cup)
- Cherry tomatoes (1 cup)
- Large avocado (1)
- Pine nuts (.25 cup)
- Rice vinegar (1 tbsp.)
- Grapeseed or olive oil (2 tbsp.)
- Black pepper & salt (as desired)

How To Prepare

1. Rinse and dry the arugula leaves, grate the cheese, and slice the cherry tomatoes into halves. Peel and slice the avocado.
2. Combine the arugula, pine nuts, tomatoes, oil, vinegar, and cheese.
3. Sprinkle with a dusting of pepper and salt as desired.
4. Cover and toss to mix. Portion onto plates with the avocado slices and serve.

Avocado Mediterranean Salad

Servings Provided: 4-6

Preparation & Cooking Time: 15 minutes

What You Need

- Roma tomato (2 large)
- Seedless - English/hothouse cucumber - diced (half of 1)
- Shallot (1)
- Avocado (2) + Fresh lemon juice (as needed over avocado pieces)
- Pitted Kalamata olives (.25 cup/as desired)
- Optional: Halloumi cheese (3-4 oz. or 85-110 g)
- Basil leaves (10-15)
- Olive oil (only if using halloumi)

    The Vinaigrette:

- Lemon (1)
- Olive oil (.25 cup)
- Garlic (1 clove)
- Za'atar spice (1.5 tsp. + more to sprinkle)
- Pepper & salt

How To Prepare

1. Do the prep. Slice the shallot, then dice the cucumber and tomatoes. Peel, pit, and dice the avocado. Dice the cheese into small cubes and thinly slice the basil. Gather the basil and thinly slice/chiffonade. Zest and juice the lemon.
2. Add the vinaigrette fixings into a mason jar, cover tightly, and shake thoroughly till well-combined. Set aside for now.
3. Toss the salad fixings – minus the basil and cheese. Pour the vinaigrette and gently toss the salad. Add the basil and give one very quick toss.
4. If adding halloumi cheese, mix the cubes with oil (1-2 tbsp.) in a mixing container. Toss to coat the cheese with the EVOO.
5. Warm an indoor griddle using a medium-temperature setting. Add the cheese cubes - grill for two to three minutes - turning over on all sides until lightly browned and nice char marks appear.
6. Add the grilled Halloumi to the salad and serve promptly.

Brown Rice Salad

Servings Provided: 6

Preparation & Cooking Time: 55-60 minutes

What You Need

- Uncooked brown rice (1.5 cups)
- Water (3 cups)
- Bell pepper (1 red)
- Frozen green peas (1 cup)
- Raisins (.5 cup)
- Sweet onion - ex. Vidalia (¼ of 1)
- Kalamata olives (.25 cup)
- Vegetable oil (.5 cup)
- Balsamic vinegar (.25 cup)
- Dijon mustard (1.25 tsp.)
- Black pepper & salt (as desired)
- Feta cheese (.25 cup)

How To Prepare

1. Prep the veggies. Thaw the peas. Thinly slice the pepper – then, chop the onion and olives. Prepare the rice and water using the high heat temperature setting. Once boiling, lower the setting to med-low and put a top on the pot. Simmer it for 45 to 50 minutes.
2. Whisk the mustard with the vinegar and oil for the dressing.
3. Combine the olives, onion, raisins, peppers, and peas in a mixing bowl.
4. Mix it all with a portion of pepper and salt. Garnish it with feta and serve.

Chickpea Salad

Servings Provided: 4

Preparation & Cooking Time: 20-25 minutes

What You Need
- Cooked chickpeas (15 oz. or 430 g)
- Roma tomato (1)
- Green bell pepper (half of 1 medium)
- Fresh parsley (1 tbsp.)
- White onion (1 small)
- Garlic (.5 tsp.)
- Lemon (1 juiced)

How To Prepare
1. Chop the tomato, green pepper, and onion. Mince the garlic.
2. Combine each of the fixings into a salad bowl and toss well.
3. Place a layer of plastic or foil over the salad. Pop it in the fridge till it's chilled (15 min. minimum).
4. Serve when ready.

Fig & Goat Cheese Salad

Servings Provided: 1

Preparation & Cooking Time: 5-10 minutes

What You Need

- Mixed salad greens (2 cups)
- Dried figs (4)
- Crumbled fresh goat cheese (1 oz./28 g)
- Slivered almonds – toasted is best (1.5 tbsp.)
- Olive oil - EVOO (2 tsp.)
- Honey (.5 tsp.)
- Balsamic vinegar (2 tsp.)
- Salt and pepper (1 dash as desired - for each)

How To Prepare

1. Prepare the salad by combining the greens, figs, cheese, and almonds in a large dish.
2. Mix the vinegar, oil, salt, pepper, and honey together for the dressing.
3. You can make this tasty treat ahead of the meal - for up to 24 hours. Just add the dressing and serve.

Delightful Quinoa Salad

Servings Provided: 4

Preparation & Cooking Time: 2 hours 40 minutes

What You Need

- Quinoa (1 cup - uncooked)
- Red wine vinegar (.33 or 1/3 cup)
- Water (2 cups)
- Olive oil (.25 cup)
- Red onion (1 small)
- Red pepper (1)
- Kalamata olives (.5 cup)
- Lemon (1 juiced)
- Chopped fresh cilantro (.5 cup)
- Black pepper (.5 tsp.)
- Salt (1 tsp.)
- Feta cheese (.5 cup - crumbled)
- Roma tomatoes (2)

How To Prepare

1. First do the prep. Dice the tomatoes, onions, and peppers.
2. Over medium heat, prepare the water to boil and toss in the quinoa. Reduce the temperature setting and continue to simmer for 15-20 minutes. The water should be completely absorbed. Fluff and cool for five minutes.
3. Add the vinegar and oil—as the quinoa comes to room temperature.
4. Blend in the tomatoes, onion, olives, red peppers, cilantro, pepper, and salt. Gently blend and add the feta cheese.
5. Chill in the fridge for about two hours so the flavors can intertwine.
6. Before serving, give it a drizzle of lemon juice.

Fruit Salad With Honey-Mint Sauce

Servings Provided: 2

Preparation & Cooking Time: 15 minutes (+) chilling time

What You Need
- Apple (half of 1)
- Banana (¼ of 1)
- Blueberries (.25 cup)
- Raspberries (.25 cup)
- Strawberries (.25 cup)
- Plum (half of 1)
- Peach (half of 1)
- Mint (1 tbsp.)
- Mint-flavored tea bag (1)
- Lemon juice (.25 tbsp.)
- Honey (.5 tbsp.)
- Water (.33 or 1/3 cup)

How To Prepare
1. Peel and cube the apple. Remove the pits from the plum and peach. Chop the mint and remove the banana peeling.
2. Pour the water into a small saucepan. Once it boils, add the tea bag, juice, and honey. Simmer for a minute or two until it's like you like it. Let it slightly cool.
3. Mix the fruit in a container and pour the mixture into the bowl. Stir and chill in the refrigerator.
4. Serve with a sprinkle of fresh mint.

Greek Tabbouleh Salad

Servings Provided: 4

Preparation & Cooking Time: 40 minutes

What You Need

- Hot water (2-inches in a bowl)
- Medium bulgur (.75 cup/4 oz.)
- Lemon juice - fresh (3 tbsp.)
- Olive oil (3 tbsp.)
- Seedless cucumber (1 @ 1-2-inches - diced)
- Halved cherry tomatoes (.5 pint)
- Scallions (2 thinly sliced)
- Crumbled feta (.5 cup/3 oz.)
- Pitted olives (.25 cup)
- Flat-leaf parsley (.25 cup)
- Mint (.25 cup)
- Pepper & Salt as desired

How To Prepare

1. Use a covered container and add the bulgur in two inches of hot water. Let it soak 20 minutes. Drain and press firmly - removing the excess water. Clean the dish.
2. Whisk the oil and juice and add the bulgur, cucumber, tomatoes, olives, feta, mint, and parsley.
3. Give it a shake of pepper and salt – tossing well.
4. Let it absorb the fixings for about ten minutes. Toss and serve!
5. You can also wait about eight hours to serve if you want to make it ahead of time.

Greek Yogurt With Cucumber & Dill Salad

Servings Provided: 6

Preparation & Cooking Time: 20 minutes

What You Need

- Dried dill (1 tbsp.)
- Garlic powder (.25 tsp.)
- Salt (.5 tsp.)
- Sugar (.5 tsp.)
- Black pepper (.25 tsp.)
- Apple cider vinegar (1 tbsp.)
- Greek yogurt (4 tbsp.)
- Cucumbers (4 large)

How To Prepare

1. Combine all of the fixings except for the cucumber in a mixing dish. Whisk until well combined.
2. Slice and add the cucumbers, gently tossing.
3. Chill the salad for about 10 minutes in the fridge before serving.

Honey-Walnut Salad With Feta & Raisins

Servings Provided: 6

Preparation & Cooking Time: 20 minutes

What You Need

- Walnuts (1 handful)
- Natural honey (2 tbsp.)

    The Salad:

- Raisins (.5 cup)
- Parmesan cheese (4 oz./110 g)
- Baby spinach (1.5 lb./680 g)
- Large apple (1 cut into pieces)
- Honey walnuts ↑ (1 cup)

    The Dressing:

- Olive oil (2 tsp.)
- Cranberry juice (2 tsp.)
- Honey (2 tbsp.)
- Mustard (2 tsp.)
- Rice vinegar (2 tsp.)
- Black pepper & salt (as desired)

How To Prepare

1. Set the oven temperatures to 325° Fahrenheit/163° Celsius.
2. Take a pan and pour in the walnuts. Pour the walnuts into a pan and coat them with honey. Pop them in the oven (15 min.). Transfer them to the countertop to cool.
3. Toss all of the fixings in a small mixing container for the salad. Add the walnuts.
4. Mix all the dressing fixings in a jar - thoroughly shake.
5. Add the dressing to the salad and serve.

Lebanese Lentil Salad

Servings Provided: 6

Preparation & Cooking Time: 50 minutes

What You Need
- Green lentils (1 cup)
- Olive oil (4 tbsp. - as needed)
- Garlic (10-12 cloves or to taste)
- Fresh mint (.75 cup)
- Fresh parsley (.75 cup)
- Ground allspice (.25 tsp.)
- Fresh-squeezed lemon juice (4 tbsp.)
- Ground cumin (1.5 tsp.)
- Salt & pepper (as desired)

How To Prepare
1. Remove any broken lentils and rinse them thoroughly. Pour them into a saucepan with three cups of water. Wait for it to boil and cook until the lentils are succulent (25-30 min.).
2. While the lentils cook, mince the garlic.
3. Warm a pan and heat two to three tablespoons of oil. Toss in the garlic. Sauté it using the low-temperature setting (7-8 min.). Turn off the heat.
4. Finely chop the mint and parsley.
5. Whisk the lemon juice with oil (2 tbsp.), cumin, and allspice.
6. After the lentils are tender, drain the liquids, and empty them into a mixing container.
7. Reheat the garlic pan and pour in the lemon juice dressing mixture to heat it for about one minute. Add the dressing with the lentils, fresh herbs, salt, and pepper.
8. Serve the salad either hot or at room temperature.
9. Serve it for up to two days with a spritz of fresh lemon juice to your liking.

Sweet & Spicy Jicama Salad

Servings Provided: 6

Preparation & Cooking Time: 40 minutes

What You Need
- Navel oranges (2)
- Sweet yellow peppers (3 small)
- Large jicama (1)
- Large red bell pepper (1)
- Hothouse cucumber (half of 1)
- Sweet orange peppers (2 small)
- Radishes (4)
- Thai chili peppers (3)
- Jalapeno pepper (half of 1)
- Cilantro (half of 1)
- Lemon (1 - juiced)
- Black pepper (as desired)

How To Prepare
1. You'll love this one (and it is vegan-friendly).
2. Prep the veggies and toss them in a mixing bowl. (Peel and julienne the jicama. Cut the oranges and red pepper into chunks. Dice the cucumber and chili peppers. Slice the yellow and orange peppers. Chop the cilantro jalapeno, and thinly slice the radishes.)
3. Cover the dish. Marinate for about half an hour and serve.

Tuna Antipasto Salad

Servings Provided: 4

Preparation & Cooking Time: 15 minutes

What You Need

- Beans – ex. chickpeas or kidney beans (15-19 oz./430-540 g can)
- Chunk light tuna – water-packed (2 cans @ 6 oz./170 g each)
- Red onion (.5 cup)
- Bell pepper (1 red - large)
- Chopped fresh parsley – divided (.5 cup)
- Capers (4 tsp.)
- Rosemary (1.5 tsp.)
- Lemon juice – divided (.5 tsp.)
- Olive oil (4 tbsp.)
- Salt (.25 tsp.)
- Black pepper (1 dash or as desired)
- Mixed salad greens (8 cups)

How To Prepare

1. Rinse the capers and beans. Dice the onion, pepper, rosemary, and parsley.
2. Mix the tuna, beans, peppers, parsley, onion, capers, rosemary, oil (2 tbsp.), and lemon juice (1/4 of a cup).
3. Sprinkle with pepper and combine the rest of the juice, oil, and salt.
4. Add the greens and toss to serve.

Tuna Spinach Salad

Servings Provided: 1

Preparation & Cooking Time: 10 minutes

What You Need

- Tahini (1.5 tbsp.)
- Water (1.5 tbsp.)
- Chunk light tuna in water (5 oz./140 g can)
- Lemon juice (1.5 tbsp.)
- Pitted Kalamata olives (4)
- Parsley (2 tbsp.)
- Feta cheese (2 tbsp.)
- Baby spinach (2 cups)
- Orange (1 medium)

How To Prepare

1. Drain the tuna and chop the olives.
2. Whisk the water, juice, and tahini in a mixing container. Then blend in the rest of the fixings – stirring well to combine.
3. Serve over the baby spinach with the orange peeled and sliced on the side.

Watermelon-Olive- Feta & Caper Salad

Servings Provided: 6

Preparation & Cooking Time: 8-10 minutes

What You Need

- Olive oil (2 tbsp. + .25 cup)
- Capers (.25 cup
- Pitted – halved Kalamata olives (.33 or 1/3 cup)
- Black pepper (as desired)
- Sherry vinegar (1.5 tbsp.)
- Watermelon (5 cups)
- Fresh basil & mint (.5 cup each)
- Feta cheese – coarsely crumbled (.66 or 2/3 cup)
- Lightly toasted almonds (.25 cup)
- To Garnish: Flaky sea salt

How To Prepare

1. Dice the watermelon into one-inch chunks. Thoroughly rinse the capers.
2. Heat oil (2 tbsp.) in a small pan using a high-temperature setting on the stovetop. Pat the capers dry and add to the oil, sautéing for one to three minutes.
3. Transfer the crispy capers to a towel and discard the oil.
4. Whisk the rest of the fixings with the rest of the oil, vinegar, and pepper.
5. Dice the watermelon and mix it in with the thinly sliced mint and basil.
6. Gently toss and add to the serving dishes. Sprinkle with the almonds, feta, and capers. Give it a sprinkling of sea salt.

Wrap & Flatbread Options

Garden Wrap

Servings Provided: 4

Preparation & Cooking Time: 15-20 minutes

What You Need

- Tomatoes (2)
- Greek yogurt (1 cup)
- Chopped of each:
    - Cilantro (1 tbsp.)
    - Chives (1 tbsp.)
    - Fresh mint (1 tbsp.)
- Cooked peas (.5 cup)
- Red onion (.5 cup)
- Cucumber (1.5 cups)
- Shredded/sliced carrots (1.5 cups)
- Lavash* (4 sheets)
- Kosher salt (.5 tsp./to taste)

How To Prepare

1. Cut the tomatoes in half and slice them thin.
2. Mix the salt, yogurt, and herbs in a small dish.
3. In another medium dish, slice, and mix the cucumber, carrots, red onion, and cooked peas.
4. Place one lavash sheet on countertop or platter and add approximately ¼ of the mix of yogurt down the center, a layer of tomatoes, ¼ carrot mix, and fold/roll to one side of the flatbread.
5. Use several toothpicks to secure the ends. Cut it in half and repeat with the remainder of the products.
6. *Note: Lavash is a Mediterranean soft flatbread.

Kale & Hummus Wrap

Servings Provided: 1

Preparation & Cooking Time: 10 minutes

What You Need

- Whole grain tortilla - no-sugar or additives (1 medium)
- Prepared hummus (.25 cup)
- Dino kale (1 cup or 1 large leaf - cleaned & massaged for better texture)
- Chopped tomatoes (.25 cup)
- Chopped yellow onions (.25 cup)
- Avocado (half of 1 medium)

How To Prepare

1. Make the tortilla on cutting board - spread the hummus over its top.
2. Layer the rest of the ingredients.
3. Roll up like a burrito and secure the two ends with toothpicks.
4. Slice in half and remove the toothpicks before serving.

Mediterranean Flatbread

Servings Provided: 2

Preparation & Cooking Time: 20-25 minutes

What You Need

- Grape tomatoes (.33 or 1/3 cup
- Roasted red peppers (.25 cup)
- Kalamata olives (.25 cup)
- Marinated artichoke hearts (.25 cup)
- Lime juice (1 tsp.)
- Roasted garlic (4-5 cloves)
- Parsley (2 tsp.)
- Feta cheese (1-2 oz. or 28-56 g)
- Olive oil (1 tbsp.)
- Pre-made pizza dough (half of a ball)

How To Prepare

1. Do the prep. Slice the olives and tomatoes into halves. Chop or dice the peppers, artichoke hearts, and garlic.
2. Toss the garlic with the olives, tomatoes, artichokes, lime juice, parsley, and roasted red peppers in a mixing container.
3. Set the oven to 450° Fahrenheit/232° Celsius.
4. Prepare a rectangular dish with parchment paper or oil.
5. Roll out the dough to 8 by 12-inch/20 by 30-cm size. Arrange in the pan and rub with the oil. Add the feta as desired.
6. Bake 12-15 minutes until crispy.
7. Slice and garnish with the parsley.

Chapter 4: Mediterranean Soup Specialties

Barley-Mushroom Soup

Servings Provided: 4

Prep & Cooking Time: 1 hour 20 minutes

What You Need
- Olive oil
- Baby Bella mushrooms (16 oz. or 450 g)
- Kosher salt
- Yellow onion (1)
- Garlic cloves (4)
- Celery (2 stalks)
- Carrot (1)
- White mushrooms (8 oz. or 230 g)
- Crushed tomatoes (.5 cup - canned)
- Black pepper
- Coriander (1 tsp.)
- Smoked paprika (.5 to .75 tsp.)
- Cumin (.5 tsp.)
- Broth - beef or vegetable – l. s. (6 cups)
- Pearl barley (1 cup)
- Parsley (.5 cup - tightly packed)

How To Prepare
1. First, prep the veggies. Clean, halve, and slice the baby Bella mushrooms. Clean and chop the white mushrooms. Chop the carrots, celery, garlic, onions, and parsley. Rinse the barley.
2. Prepare a Dutch oven to warm the oil using a med-high temperature setting till it's shimmering - not smoking.

3. Next, toss in the baby Bella mushrooms and cook till the mushrooms soften and are lightly browned (5 min.). Transfer them to a holding container for now.
4. In the same pan, add a tiny bit of oil. Toss and sauté the onions, garlic, celery, carrots, chopped white mushrooms, pepper, and salt using a med-high setting (4-5 min.)
5. Now, fold in the crushed tomatoes and spices (smoked paprika, coriander, & cumin). Simmer – stirring often (3 min.).
6. Mix in the broth and barley. Let it reach to a rolling boil for about five minutes, then reduce the temperature setting. Cover and simmer using a low-temperature setting till the barley is tender and thoroughly cooked (45 min.).
7. Add the cooked Bella mushrooms to the pot, stirring to combine. Simmer five minutes until the mushrooms are thoroughly heated. Garnish with parsley to serve.

Egg & Lemon Greek Soup

Servings Provided: 8-10

Preparation & Cooking Time: 25 minutes

What You Need
- Converted rice (.25 cup)
- Pepper (.5 tsp.)
- Eggs (2)
- Chicken stock (6 cups)
- Salt (1 tsp.)
- Lemon (1 juiced)

How To Prepare
1. Warm the chicken stock in a big soup pot. Once simmering, blend in the rice and cook (15 min.).
2. Mix the lemon juice and eggs - slowly add it to the simmering broth. Don't boil to prevent curdling. The egg cooks instantly.
3. Season with pepper and salt to serve.

Homemade Vegetable Soup

Servings Provided: 6

Preparation & Cooking Time: 45 minutes

What You Need

- Olive oil - ex. - Private Reserve Greek EVOO (1 tbsp./as needed)
- Baby Bella mushrooms (8 oz./230 g)
- Flat-leaf (1 bunch)
- Yellow/red onion (1 medium)
- Garlic (2 cloves)
- Celery (2 ribs)
- Carrots (2)
- Zucchini (2 medium)
- Golden potatoes (2)
- Turmeric powder (.5 tsp.)
- Ground coriander (1 tsp.)
- Sweet paprika (.5 tsp.)
- Dry thyme (.5 tsp.)
- Black pepper & salt (as desired)
- Whole peeled tomatoes (32-oz./910 g can)
- Chickpeas - rinsed and drained (15-oz./430 g can)
- Bay leaves (2)
- Low-sodium vegetable/chicken broth (6 cups)
- Lime (1 zested & juiced)
- Optional: Toasted pine nuts (.33 or 1/3 cup)

How To Prepare

1. Rinse and drain the beans into a colander. Remove the tops from the zucchini and slice them into rounds or dice them to bite-sized pieces.
2. Prepare a large pot to warm one tablespoon of oil using the med-high temperature setting until shimmering - but not smoking. Slice and add the mushrooms and sauté them for three to five minutes, stirring regularly. Remove from the pot and set aside from now.

3. Prepare the parsley. Wash and dry the parsley and separate the stems to chop.
4. Add more olive oil, if needed, and heat the pan. Chop and add the parsley stems (stems only). Peel and dice the garlic, carrots, onions, celery, and small potatoes. Add in the zucchini.
5. Next, sprinkle in the spices, pepper, and salt. Simmer until the veggies have started to soften (7 min.).
6. Fold in the chickpeas, tomatoes, bay leaves, and broth. Boil for five minutes and lower the temperature setting to med-low. Partly cover the pot to simmer (15 min.).
7. Fold in the sauteed mushrooms and simmer until heated. Mix in the lime zest, parsley leaves, and lime juice.
8. Place the pot on a cool burner and discard the bay leaves.
9. Serve with a garnish of toasted pine nuts, your favorite crusty bread, a few lime wedges, and crushed red pepper.

Lentil Greek Soup

Servings Provided: 4

Preparation & Cooking Time: 1 hour 20 minutes

What You Need

- Brown lentils (8 oz. or 230 g)
- Carrot (1 large)
- Garlic (1 tbsp.)
- Onion (1)
- Olive oil (.25 cup/as needed)
- Water (1 quart)
- Crushed - dried rosemary & oregano (1 pinch of each)
- Tomato paste (1 tbsp.)
- Black pepper and salt (as desired)
- Bay leaves (2)
- Optional: Vinegar – ex. red wine (1 tsp.)

How To Prepare

1. Chop the garlic, onion, and carrot.
2. Cook the lentils in a saucepan covered with water by about one inch. Once the beans start boiling, cook them until tender (10 min.). Dump them into a colander to drain.
3. Warm the oil in a pan using a medium-temperature setting. Sauté the onion, carrot, and garlic (5 min.)
4. Add the water, lentils, oregano, bay leaves, pepper, salt, and rosemary. Once boiling, decrease the temperature setting to med-low and cover to cook (10 min.).
5. Now stir in the tomato paste.
6. Place a lid on the pot to simmer (30-40 min.). Add water as needed.
7. When ready to serve, drizzle with the vinegar and oil (1 tsp.).

Meatball Soup

Servings Provided: 6

Preparation & Cooking Time: 1 hour 10 minutes

What You Need

- Olive oil - divided (4 tsp.)
- Lean ground turkey (1 lb. or 450 g)
- Italian seasoning, divided (2.5 tsp.)
- Paprika (.25 tsp.)
- Black pepper - coarsely ground & salt - divided (.25 tsp. each)
- Fresh baby carrots (15)
- Celery (2 ribs)
- Small onion (1)
- Chicken broth - reduced-sodium (14.5 oz./410 g can)
- Cannellini beans (15 oz./430 g can)
- Italian diced tomatoes (14.5 oz. can - undrained)
- Fresh green beans (.75 cup)
- Chopped cabbage (.75 cup)
- Mozzarella cheese - part-skim (3 tbsp. - shredded)

How To Prepare

1. Rinse and drain the beans in a colander.
2. Combine the turkey with 1.5 teaspoons Italian seasoning, and paprika. Lastly add the salt and pepper (1/8 teaspoon each). Break the mixture into 36 meatballs.
3. Prep a frying pan using a spritz of cooking oil spray. Brown the meatballs in batches in two teaspoons oil until done (center not pink). Transfer them to a holding container.
4. Spritz a saucepan with cooking oil spray. Add and warm the remainder of the oil. Chop and sauté the carrots, celery, and onion until tender.
5. Mix in the tomatoes, cannellini beans, broth, green beans, cabbage, remaining Italian seasoning, pepper, and salt.
6. Wait for it to boil and lower the temperature setting.

7. Add the meatballs and simmer, uncovered, until green beans are tender (15-20 min.). Sprinkle the soup with cheese and serve.

Mediterranean Stew

Servings Provided: 6

Preparation & Cooking Time: 7 hours 15 minutes

What You Need

- Chickpeas – no-salt - divided (15 oz. or 430 g can)
- Lacinato kale (1 bunch - about 8 cups or 1.9 L)
- Fire-roasted diced tomatoes – no-salt (2 cans @ 14 oz./400 g each)
- Vegetable broth – l. s. (3 cups)
- Olive oil (3 tbsp.)
- Garlic cloves (4)
- Onion (1 cup)
- Carrot (.75 cup)
- Salt (.75 tsp.)
- Red pepper - crushed (.5 tsp.)
- Black pepper (.25 tsp.)
- Basil leaves – freshly torn
- Oregano - dried (1 tsp.)
- Lemon juice (1 tbsp.)
- Optional: Lemon wedges (6)
- Also Needed: 4-quart slow cooker

How To Prepare

1. Rinse and drain the chickpeas into a colander. Coarsely chop the onion and carrot.
2. Mince and add the garlic with the broth, tomatoes, onion, carrot, oregano, salt, crushed red pepper, and pepper into the cooker. Securely close the lid and set the timer on the low-temperature setting (6 hr.).

3. Measure ¼ cup of the cooking liquid from the cooker into a small bowl. Add chickpeas (2 tbsp.) and mash them until they're smooth.
4. Remove the stems and chop the kale. Add the mashed chickpeas, kale, lemon juice, and remaining whole chickpeas to the cooker's mixture. Stir and put the lid back on the cooker and set the timer for ½ hour using a low-temperature setting.
5. Portion the stew evenly into six bowls and add a spritz of oil.
6. Garnish with basil. Serve with lemon wedges, if desired.

Parmesan Soup - Gluten-Free

Servings Provided: 6

Preparation & Cooking Time: 35 minutes

What You Need
- Butter (8 tbsp.)
- Black pepper & salt (as desired)
- Onion sliced (half of 1 - 55 g)
- Leek sliced (half of 1 - 44.5 g)
- Cauliflower chopped (1 head or 575 g)
- Vegetable broth (2 cups + 1 bouillon cube)
- water depending on consistency (2-3 cups/500 ml)
- Thyme chopped (2 tbsp.)
- Parmesan cheese (1 cup)

How To Prepare
1. Melt some butter (2 tbsp.) in a big soup pot.
2. Measure and combine the salt, leek, and onion in the pot. Sauté the onion until it's translucent and softened.
3. Mix in half of the cauliflower, the broth, four tablespoons butter, and two cups of water to the pot. Simmer until cauliflower is tender and falling apart (10-15 min.).
4. Add cauliflower (3/4 of the remaining) to the pot. Continue cooking.

5. Melt two tablespoons butter with the thyme and the rest of the cauliflower.
6. Gently stir as the butter starts browning.
7. After the cauliflower is tender, carefully dump it into a blender. Add the parmesan cheese.
8. Blend the cauliflower mixture until it's incorporated and creamy smooth. Add more water as needed to adjust the consistency of the soup. Mix it a bit more.
9. Serve it with the florets and a spritz of browned butter.
10. You will have 240 calories per serving with 20 g of fat and 3 g of net carbs!

Persian Chilled Cucumber Soup

Servings Provided: 6

Preparation & Cooking Time: 10 minutes

What You Need
- Toasted walnut hearts (.5 cup)
- Plain yogurt - not Greek (2 cups)
- Water (1.5 cups)
- Seedless English cucumber (1 to 1.5 cups - chopped + a few slices to serve)
- Chopped fresh herbs - parsley, basil, dill, mint (1 cup)
- Gold raisins (.5 cup)
- Salt
- Sumac (.75 tsp. + more for later)

How To Prepare
1. Whisk the iced water with the yogurt. Stir in finely chopped cucumbers, herbs, raisins, toasted walnuts, sumac, and salt.
2. Put a top on the container and chill for about one hour.
3. When ready, divide chilled cucumber soup into four serving bowls.
4. Sprinkle more sumac over the tops and add a few cucumber slices to each serving.
5. Enjoy with your favorite toasted bread or pita.

White Bean Chili – Instant Pot

Servings Provided: 8

Preparation & Cooking Time: Varies or 2 hours

What You Need

- Vegetable oil (2 tbsp.)
- Chicken breasts (1.5 lb./680 g)
- Onion (1 medium)
- Garlic (4 cloves)
- Green enchilada sauce (28 oz./790 g can)
- Dry beans - Great Northern (2 cups)
- Vegetable broth (2 cups)
- Undrained green chiles (2 cans @ 4 oz./110 g cans)
- Oregano (1 tbsp.)
- Cumin (1 tsp.)
- The Garnish: Monterey Jack cheese blend - cheddar (1 cup)

How To Prepare

1. Dice the chicken into 0.5-inch cubes. Mince the garlic and onion. Chop the chiles. Sort and rinse the beans.
2. Prepare the oil in the Instant Pot using the sauté function. Toss in the diced chicken and sauté for five to seven minutes.
3. Toss in the garlic and onion to sauté for five minutes.
4. Pour in the beans, broth, enchilada sauce, green chiles, oregano, and cumin into the cooker.
5. Securely lock the top and program the timer for 45 minutes using high pressure.
6. After the cycle is complete, natural-release the built-up pressure (25 min.). The beans will continue to cook.
7. At that point, open the top and serve with the cilantro and sprinkle of cheese.

Chapter 5: Mediterranean Seafood Specialties

Frozen Italian Fish - Instant Pot

Servings Provided: 4

Preparation & Cooking Time: 20-25 minutes

What You Need
- Water (.25 cup)
- Whitefish fillets (4 frozen – halved @ 3-4 oz. or 85-110 g each)
- Cherry tomatoes (12)
- Black olives (12-14)
- Marinated baby capers (2 tbsp.)
- Roasted sliced red peppers (.33 cup)
- Olive oil (2 tbsp.)
- Salt (.5 tsp.)
- Chili flakes (a pinch)
- Optional: Freshly chopped basil/parsley

How To Prepare
1. Pour water into the Instant Pot. If the fish is frozen, use ¼ cup. Add the fish and the rest of the fixings. Spritz it with oil, sea salt, and chili flakes.
2. Securely close the lid, set the timer for four minutes using the high-pressure setting.
3. At that time, natural-release the pressure (7-8 min.) and open the lid.
4. Transfer fish to a platter, adding the broth, and cooked fixings over the top.
5. Serve with a dusting of basil or parsley.

Herbed Salmon

Servings Provided: 4

Preparation & Cooking Time: 25 to 30 minutes

What You Need

- Kosher salt (1 tsp.)
- Chili powder (.5 tsp.)
- Brown sugar (1 tbsp.)
- Salmon fillet – boneless (1.5-2 lb./680-910 g)
- Marinade (.25 cup)

How To Prepare

1. Heat the oven at 375° Fahrenheit or 191° Celsius.
2. Combine the dry fixings and rub the mix over the salmon.
3. Pour in the marinade for it to bake (20 min.). Serve when it's ready.

Moroccan Fish Favorite

Servings Provided: 12

Preparation & Cooking Time: 50 minutes

What You Need
- Vegetable oil (1 tbsp.)
- Onion (1)
- Garlic (1 clove)
- Garbanzo beans (15 oz./430 g can)
- Red bell peppers (2)
- Large carrot (1)
- Tomatoes (3)
- Olives (4)
- Fresh parsley (.25 cup)
- Ground cumin (.25 cup)
- Paprika (3 tbsp.)
- Chicken bouillon granules (2 tbsp.)
- Cayenne pepper (1 tsp.)
- Salt (as desired)
- Tilapia fillets (5 lb./2.3 kg.)

How To Prepare
1. Finely chop the garlic, onion, tomatoes, olives, and parsley. Thoroughly rinse the garbanzo beans in a colander and drain. Slice the carrots and bell peppers.
2. Warm the oil in a big skillet (medium temp). Toss in the garlic and onions to sauté until softened (5 min.).
3. Mix in the bell peppers, tomatoes, carrots, olives, and beans.
4. Simmer for about five additional minutes. Sprinkle with the paprika, cumin, parsley, chicken bouillon, and the cayenne.
5. Dust with the salt, stir the vegetables, and lastly the fish. Add water to cover the fish.
6. Set the temperature to low. Cook until the fish are flaky or about 40 minutes.

Pan Seared Mahi-Mahi in Tomato-Mascarpone Sauce

Servings Provided: 2

Preparation & Cooking Time: 20 minutes

What You Need

- Mahi-mahi (2 fillets)
- Mascarpone (4 oz./110 g)
- Dill (2 tbsp.)
- Sugar-free tomato paste (2 tbsp.)
- Pepper & salt (.5 tsp. each)
- Olive oil (2 tbsp.)
- Lemon juice (1 tbsp.)

How To Prepare

1. Chop the dill and set it aside.
2. Warm the oil in a skillet using a medium-temperature setting.
3. Dust the fish with pepper and salt, then add to the frying pan.
4. Sauté them for five minutes per side, turning once.
5. Prepare the sauce by placing the mascarpone, tomato paste, lemon juice & dill in a saucepan to gently heat – stirring till thoroughly blended.
6. Empty the sauce over the fish in the pan and simmer (2 min.).
7. Serve with green vegetables or a salad.

Pan-Seared Salmon & Asparagus

Servings Provided: 2

Preparation & Cooking Time: 25 minutes

What You Need

- Fresh salmon fillets skin removed (2 @ 4-6 oz. or 110-170 g)
- Olive oil - divided (.25 cup)
- Dijon mustard (.5 tsp.)
- Unsalted butter (1 tbsp.)
- Thick asparagus spears (8 trimmed)
- Lemon juice - fresh (4 tsp.)
- Shallot (1 minced)
- Fresh basil (2 tsp. - minced)
- Black pepper and kosher salt (as desired)

How To Prepare

1. Warm a skillet (med-high temp) to warm the oil (1 tbsp.).
2. While the pan is heating, dry the salmon fillets with several paper towels and dust each side with pepper and salt.
3. Prepare the fillets until they are brown and crispy on the first side (4-5 min.). Use a pancake turner and carefully flip the fillets over.
4. Lower the temperature setting to medium and continue cooking (3-5 min.). Check the fillets every minute or so by piercing it with a fork until the thickest part flakes through the entire thickness.
5. Transfer the pan to the countertop and place the fillets onto a serving platter. Cover loosely with a lid or piece of foil to keep warm.
6. Use a paper towel and carefully wipe out the pan. Add one tablespoon butter to the pan. Once melted, add the asparagus in a single layer with a dash of salt.
7. Cover and cook the asparagus using the medium-temperature setting for about five minutes or until they are bright green and just starting to get tender. Uncover and raise the temperature to med-high. Continue cooking the spears till they're crispy and tender (2-3 min.).
8. Meanwhile, add three tablespoons of oil, lemon juice, shallots, basil, mustard and a dash of pepper and salt to a small mason jar and shake well.
9. Add the asparagus to the platter with the fish, drizzle the dressing on the fish and serve promptly.

Pan-Seared Sea Bass

Servings Provided: 2

Preparation & Cooking Time: 15 minutes

What You Need

- Chilean sea bass (12 oz. or 340 g)
- Garlic (.5 tbsp.)
- Butter (.25 cup)
- Olive oil (2 tbsp.)
- Salt (as needed)

How To Prepare

1. Let the bass sit on the countertop about ½ hour before cooking.
2. Mince the garlic and toss in into a saucepan with butter to sauté until browned.
3. Add a bit of oil to another pan to heat using a medium heat setting.
4. Dab dry and salt both sides of the bass. Add it to the skillet to cook (4 min each side).
5. Strain the garlic from the butter and pour it over the plated fish.
6. For a thicker bass, you can pop it into a 450° Fahrenheit/232° Celsius oven for a few minutes to finish cooking as desired.

Roasted Cod With Olive-Tomato-Caper Tapenade

Servings Provided: 4

Preparation & Cooking Time: 35-40 minutes

What You Need
- Capers (1 tsp.)
- Fresh oregano (1.5 tsp.)
- Shallot (1 tsp.)
- Cured olives (.25 cup)
- Cod fillet (1 lb./450 g)
- Olive oil - split (3 tsp.)
- Balsamic vinegar (1 tsp.)
- Cherry tomatoes (1 cup)
- Black pepper (.25 tsp.)

How To Prepare
1. Rinse and chop the capers and oregano. Dice the olives and shallot. Slice the tomatoes into halves.
2. Set the oven temperature setting to reach 450° Fahrenheit/232° Celsius. Lightly spritz a baking tray using a cooking oil spray.
3. Rub the fish with two teaspoons of oil and a sprinkle of pepper.
4. Bake them until they flake easily with a fork (15-20 min.)
5. Warm the rest of the oil using a medium-temperature setting in a small skillet. Fold in the shallot to sauté for about 20 seconds. Add the tomatoes and continue cooking (1.5 min.).
6. Stir in the olives and capers to sauté for about ½ minute. Pour in the vinegar and oregano.
7. Stir the mixture thoroughly and place the pan on a cool burner. Garnish the salmon using the sauce and serve.

Seared Tuna Steaks

Servings Provided: 4

Preparation & Cooking Time: 15 minutes

What You Need

- Black pepper (.125 or 1/8 tsp.)
- Ground coriander (.5 tsp.)
- Salt - divided (.5 tsp.)
- Yellow-fin tuna steaks (4 - 6-oz./170 g @ -inches thickness)
- Also Needed: Cooking spray

  The Tomato Mixture:
- Minced garlic - jar (.5 tsp.)
- Pitted Kalamata olives (12)
- Olive oil (1 tbsp.)
- Seeded tomatoes (1.5 cups)
- Lemon juice (1 tbsp.)
- Drained capers (1 tbsp.)
- Fresh parsley (3 tbsp.)
- Green onions (.25 cup)

How To Prepare

1. Use the medium-hi heat setting and place a large pan with the cooking spray added. Drizzle the fish with the pepper, coriander, and salt (1/4 tsp.) - add it to the pan.
2. Cook four minutes per side.
3. Drain the capers. Next, chop the parsley, olives, onions, and tomatoes - blend the remainder of the ingredients. Garnish the fish with the tomato mixture and serve.

Chapter 6: Mediterranean Poultry Specialties

Chicken Favorites

Baked Popcorn Chicken

Servings Provided: 8

Preparation & Cooking Time: 1 hour 10 minutes

What You Need

- Chicken thighs (1.5 lb./680 g)
- Low-fat buttermilk (2 cups)
- Garlic - smashed (3 cloves)
- Dried basil & oregano (1 tsp. each)
- Dried thyme (.5 tsp.)
- Optional: Cayenne pepper (.25 tsp.)
- Kosher salt & black pepper (as desired)
- Sour Cream & Onion Kettle Brand® Potato Chips (3 cups - crushed)
- Unsalted butter (.25 cup - melted)
- Chopped fresh parsley leaves (2 tbsp.)

How To Prepare

1. Warm the oven set to 400° Fahrenheit/204° Celsius.
2. Lightly spray a cooling rack with a spritz of nonstick baking spray and place on a baking sheet - set aside for now.
3. Trim the fat and bones from the chicken and cut it into one-inch chunks
4. Toss the chicken with buttermilk, basil, garlic, oregano, cayenne pepper, thyme, salt, and pepper - marinate for a minimum of ½ hour - thoroughly drain.

5. Prep the chicken by dabbing it into a plate of crushed potato chips until they're covered. Arrange them on the prepared baking sheet with a spritz of butter.
6. Bake until crispy and thoroughly cooked (20-25 min.), turning about halfway through the cycle.
7. Serve immediately, garnished with parsley to your liking.

Braised Chicken With the Trimmings

Servings Provided: 4

Preparation & Cooking Time: 1 hour 30 minutes

What You Need
- Butter beans (16 oz./450 g can)
- Yellow onion (1)
- Garlic (4 cloves)
- Canned artichoke hearts (10)
- Olive oil (1 tbsp.)
- Chicken legs (4 quarters)
- Black pepper (1 tbsp.)
- Red pepper flakes (.5 tsp.)
- Salt (1 tsp.)
- Chicken stock or low-sodium broth (1-quart)
- Cherry peppers (2 cups)
- Lemons - juiced (2)
- Fresh thyme sprigs (8)
- Also Needed: Dutch oven

How To Prepare
1. Dice the onion and garlic. Drain the butter beans. Drain the artichokes and cut them in half.
2. Set the oven to reach 375° Fahrenheit/191° Celsius.
3. Prepare the pan (high temp) to warm the oil.
4. Sear the chicken until browned (5 min. each side). Place them in a warm platter.
5. Add the garlic, onion, pepper flakes, salt, and black pepper to cook (1 min.). Mix in the broth and let it simmer for another minute or so. Remove from the heat.
6. Put the chicken back in the Dutch oven and add the thyme, lemon juice, cherry peppers, and artichoke hearts. Bake for about one hour.
7. Take the chicken out of the cooker and place it in a warm platter again.
8. Stir the beans into the pan with the broth and artichoke mixture.
9. Place each leg quarter in a serving dish. Add a spoon/ladle of the artichoke, bean, and broth mixture over each serving.

Chicken-Feta Burgers

Servings Provided: 6

Preparation & Cooking Time: 20 minutes

What You Need

- Reduced-fat mayonnaise (.25 cup)
- Cucumber (.25 cup)
- Garlic powder (1 tsp.)
- Chopped roasted sweet red pepper (.5 cup)
- Greek seasoning (.5 tsp.)
- Lean ground chicken (1.5 lb./680 g)
- Crumbled feta cheese (1 cup)
- Black pepper (.25 tsp.)
- Whole wheat burger buns (6 toasted)

How To Prepare

1. Heat the broiler to the oven ahead of time. Finely chop the cucumber and mix with the mayonnaise - set the dish aside.
2. Combine all of the seasonings and the red pepper for the burgers. Mix in the chicken and the cheese. Shape into (6) ½-inch thick patties.
3. Broil the burgers approximately four inches from the heat source (3-4 min. per side) to reach an internal temp of 165° Fahrenheit/74° Celsius.
4. Serve on the buns with the cucumber sauce. Top it off with tomato and lettuce if desired and serve.

Chicken Gyros With Tzatziki Sauce

Servings Provided: 4

Preparation & Cooking Time: 40 minutes

What You Need

- Pitas (4)
- Chicken breasts (4)
- Red pepper (1)
- Red onion (half of 1)
- Mediterranean seasoning/Italian seasoning (1 tbsp.)
- *Optional*: Crumbled feta cheese & lettuce

    The Sauce:
- Chopped dill (.33 cup)
- Minced garlic (4 tsp.)
- Black pepper (.125 or 1/8 tsp.)
- Salt (.5 tsp.)
- Plain Greek yogurt (2 cups)
- Cucumber (half of 1)
- Lemon juice (1.5 tbsp.)

How To Prepare

1. To prepare the chicken, pound it to a ½-inch thickness for even cooking. Thinly slice the onion and peppers.
2. You might need to use a food processor/blender for the puree. Puree each of the sauce components and place in the refrigerator. The flavors will combine as the mixture marinates.
3. Flavor the breasts with the seasoning and cook in a big pan using a medium-temperature setting (5-6 min. per side). Slice them into strips.
4. Put the pitas together and garnish as desired - folded in a 'tunnel shape' or like a sandwich to serve.

Chicken Marrakesh

Servings Provided: 8

Preparation & Cooking Time: Using low setting (4-5 hours)

What You Need

- Breast halves – no skin (2 lb./910 g)
- Cooked chickpeas - 15 oz./430 g)
- Carrots (2 large)
- Sweet potatoes (2 large)
- Diced tomatoes (14.5 oz./410 g)
- Garlic (1 tsp.)
- White onion (1 medium)
- Salt (1 tsp.)
- Turmeric (.5 tsp.)
- Dried parsley (1 tsp.)
- Cinnamon (.5 tsp.)
- Ground cumin (.5 tsp.)
- Black pepper (.5 tsp.)
- Suggested Slow Cooker Size: 6-quart

How To Prepare

1. Lightly grease the slow cooker.
2. Slice the chicken into two-inch pieces. Peel and dice the sweet potatoes, carrots, and white onions. Mince the garlic.
3. Stir or whisk the parsley, cumin, turmeric, black pepper, and salt in a mixing container.
4. Add the remainder of the fixings into the greased cooker.
5. Secure the lid on the cooker and set the timer for four to five hours. The chicken should be done throughout, and the potatoes should be tender.
6. Serve promptly.

Chicken Souvlaki

Servings Provided: 4-6

Preparation & Cooking Time: 20 minutes

What You Need

- Lemon juice (2 tbsp.)
- Nonfat Greek yogurt (14 oz./400 g)
- Freshly chopped oregano leaves (2 tsp.)
- White dry wine (.25 cup)
- Olive oil (.25 cup)
- Pepper - divided (.5 tsp.)
- Kosher salt (1 tsp.)
- Chicken breasts (2 lb./910 g)
- Garlic cloves (4 with 2 minced & 2 crushed)
- Distilled white vinegar (2 tsp.)
- Cucumber (.5 cup)

How To Prepare

1. Trim the fat and bones from the chicken and cut it into ½-inch cubes, and coarsely shred the cucumber.
2. Set the grill between 450° Fahrenheit/232° Celsius and 500° Fahrenheit/260° Celsius.
3. Blend the wine, oil, chicken, oregano, lemon juice, cloves, ¼ teaspoon of the pepper, and the salt in a mixing bowl.
4. Use eight metal skewers to prepare the chicken for cooking. Grill for approximately 10-12 minutes.
5. Remove any excess moisture from the cucumbers with paper towels and put them into a medium dish. Mix in the yogurt, garlic, vinegar, and pepper with the cucumbers.
6. Serve with warm pita bread and the chicken.

Creamy Tuscan Garlic Chicken - Keto-Adaptable

Servings Provided: 6

Preparation & Cooking Time: 25 minutes

What You Need

- Chicken breasts (1.5 lb. or 680 g)
- Heavy cream (1 cup)
- Olive oil (2 tbsp.)
- Chicken broth (.5 cup)
- Garlic powder (1 tsp.)
- Sun-dried tomatoes (.5 cup)
- Italian seasoning (1 tsp.)
- Parmesan cheese (.5 cup)
- Spinach (1 cup)

How To Prepare

1. Trim the fat and bones from the chicken and thinly slice it.
2. Prepare a big frying pan to warm the oil - cook the chicken using the med-high temperature setting until brown and the pink is gone from its center (3-5 min. each side). Transfer the chicken onto a plate.
3. Measure and add the chicken broth, heavy cream, Italian seasoning, garlic powder, and parmesan cheese to the pan.
4. Whisk it using the med-high temperature setting until it starts to thicken.
5. Chop and toss in the spinach and sundried tomatoes. Gently simmer till the spinach begins to wilt.
6. Mix the chicken back into the skillet to reheat.
7. Serve the delicious chicken over a dish of your favorite pasta.
8. For keto, you will have 368 calories and two net carbs with 25 grams of fat.

Grape & Grilled Chicken Skewers

Servings Provided: 4

Preparation & Cooking Time: 20 minutes (+) 4 hours marinating time

What You Need

Marinade Ingredients

- Olive oil - EVOO (.25 cup)
- Crushed red chili flakes (.5 tsp.)
- Garlic (2 cloves)
- Oregano & rosemary (1 tbsp. each)
- Lemon zest (1 tsp.)
- Salt (.5 tsp.)
- Chicken breast (1 lb. or 450 g)

Other Ingredients:

- Olive oil (2 tbsp.)
- Green - seedless grapes (1.75 cups)
- Fresh lemon juice (1 tbsp.)

How To Prepare

1. Do the prep by mincing the garlic, oregano, and rosemary.
2. Combine the garlic, olive oil, rosemary, oregano, and lemon zest to make the marinade. Whisk well.
3. Trim the bones and fat from the chicken and chop it into ¾-inch chunks.
4. Thread 12 skewers, alternating the grapes and chicken. Arrange them in a baking dish and marinate for four to 24 hours.
5. When ready to grill, let the excess juices drip off. Season with the salt.
6. Grill until the chicken is barbecued thoroughly, usually three to five minutes per side.
7. Lay them out on a serving tray and drizzle with some juice and oil.

Lebanese Grilled Shish Tawook – Skewers

Servings Provided: 6

Preparation & Cooking Time: 4 hours 25 minutes

What You Need

The Chicken:
- Chicken thighs (2 lb. or 910 g)
- Kosher salt

The Marinade:
- Greek yogurt - plain (.75 cup)
- Lemon (.25 cup + zest of 1 lemon)
- Olive oil (.25 cup)
- Tomato paste (2 tbsp.)
- Garlic cloves (8 minced)
- Paprika (1 tsp.)
- Ground ginger (.5 tsp.)
- Nutmeg (.5 tsp.)
- Oregano - dried (.75 tsp.)
- Allspice (1 tsp.)
- Cinnamon (.5 tsp.)
- Cayenne pepper (.5 tsp.)

How To Prepare

1. Prepare the marinade. Whisk the yogurt with the lemon juice, zest, EVOO, tomato paste, garlic, and spices in a big mixing container. Cut the chicken into chunks while removing all skin and bones.
2. Dab the chicken dry and season with salt over each side. Toss the chicken into the marinade – tossing to cover.
3. Place a top on the container and refrigerate for four to eight hours.
4. Warm the grill at medium and lightly oil the grates.
5. Thread the chicken pieces through skewers and place them single-layered onto the grill. Cover and cook for about 15 to 20 minutes, turning every five to seven minutes, until the chicken is thoroughly cooked.

Lemony Chicken Skewers

Servings Provided: 6

Preparation & Cooking Time: 4 hours 45 minutes

What You Need
- Olive oil (.25 cup)
- Lemon juice (3 tbsp.)
- Salt (1 tsp.)
- Sugar (.5 tsp.)
- Dried oregano (.25 tsp.)
- Black pepper (.25 tsp.)
- Zucchini (3 medium)
- Minced garlic (2 cloves)
- White wine vinegar (1 tbsp.)
- Lemon zest (2 tsp.)
- Medium onions (3 into wedges)
- Cherry tomatoes (12)
- Chicken breasts (1.5 lb./680 g)

How To Prepare
1. Slice the zucchini into halves - lengthwise. Then, slice them into 1.5-inch segments.
2. Remove the peel and slice the onions into wedges. Zest the lemon. Cut the chicken into 1.5-inch pieces.
3. Prepare the marinade; combine the sugar, pepper, oregano, salt, lemon zest, vinegar, lemon juice, and oil - reserving ¼ cup for basting.
4. Fold in the chicken and toss to cover.
5. Add the remainder of the marinade in a mixing container - adding the tomatoes, onions, and zucchini. Cover and pop it into the refrigerator overnight (for best results) or a minimum of four hours.
6. When ready to cook, drain, and trash the marinade.
7. Soak the wooden skewers in water.
8. Thread the chicken and veggies onto the soaked skewers.

9. Arrange the skewers on the grill. Cook them for six minutes using the medium heat setting. It's done when poked with a fork - the juices will run clear.

Lemon-Za'atar -Grilled Chicken

Servings Provided: 4

Preparation & Cooking Time: 20 minutes

What You Need
- Chicken thighs (4 @ 6-8 oz. or 170-230 g)
- Lemon zest (1 tsp.)
- Lemon (1 - sliced - 4 wedges)
- Lemon juice (2 tbsp.)
- Garlic (1 tsp.)
- Green onions (8)
- Salt & black pepper (.25 tsp. each)

How To Prepare
1. Blend the zest, oil, lemon juice, za'atar, pepper, minced garlic, and salt in a big container. Put the thighs into the mix and fully cover the surfaces.
2. Use the medium grill temperature setting ranging from 350° Fahrenheit/177° Celsius to 450° Fahrenheit/232° Celsius.
3. Arrange the chicken on the surface—skin side down (5-8 min.). Flip the thighs and continue cooking (4 min.).
4. For the last few minutes, grill the onions and lemon wedges—flipping once.

Lemon Thyme Chicken With Fingerlings

Servings Provided: 4

Preparation & Cooking Time: 40 minutes

What You Need

- Canola/olive oil – divided (4 tsp.)
- Dried thyme – divided (1 tsp.)
- Black pepper + Regular salt (.25 tsp. each)
- Fingerling or tiny new red/white potatoes (1 lb. or 450 g)
- Chicken breast halves (4 small or 1 to 1.25 lb./570 g total)
- Minced garlic (2 cloves)
- Thinly sliced lemon (1)

How To Prepare

1. Remove all of the skin and bones from the chicken. Slice the potatoes into halves – lengthwise.
2. Warm the oil (2 tsp. @ med. temp) in a frying pan and mix in the salt, pepper, and thyme (.5 tsp.).
3. When thoroughly mixed, add the potatoes, put a lid on the pan, and cook (12 min.).
4. Stir and push to one side of the skillet. Add the remainder of the oil - add the chicken and garlic. Let it cook five minutes – uncovered.
5. Flip the chicken and sprinkle with the remainder of the thyme. Arrange the slices of lemon on top and cover. Prepare until the potatoes are tender and the chicken reaches an internal temp of 170° Fahrenheit/77° Celsius and is no longer pink (7-10 min.) to serve.

Turkey Favorites

Black Olive & Feta Turkey Burgers

Servings Provided: 4

Preparation & Cooking Time: 20 minutes

What You Need
- Lean ground turkey (1 lb. or 450 g)
- Red onion (.25 cup)
- Black olives (.25 cup)
- Garlic cloves (2 - divided)
- Feta cheese - reduced-fat (1.5 oz. or 42 g)
- Lemon juice (1 tsp.)
- Black pepper (.5 tsp.)
- Dried dill - divided (2 tsp.)
- Salt (.25 tsp.)
- Nonfat plain Greek yogurt (.5 cup)

How To Prepare
1. Mince/chop the onion, olives, and garlic.
2. Mix the onion, olives, turkey, one clove of garlic, feta (4 tbsp.), dried dill (1 tsp.), salt, and pepper. Make four patties.
3. In another container, combine the feta (2 tbsp.) with the yogurt, salt, pepper, dill (1 tsp.), a garlic clove, and lemon juice.
4. Warm the grill or skillet using the med-high heat setting. Cook the burgers for five minutes on each side.
5. Serve with two tablespoons of the yogurt-feta sauce.

Turkey Bolognese Sauce

Servings Provided: 6

Preparation & Cooking Time: 3 hours 15 minutes

What You'll Need:
- EVOO - Olive oil (3 tbsp.)
- Onion (1 small)
- Celery (1 stalk)
- Carrots (2 small)
- Ground turkey/lean beef (.75 lb./340 g)
- Black pepper & kosher salt
- Whole milk (1 cup/ 250 ml)
- Ground nutmeg (.125 or 1/8 tsp.)
- Dry white wine (1 cup)
- Whole plum tomatoes – canned & diced (7 or about 1.5 cups)

How To Prepare
1. Do the prep. Chop the celery, onion, and carrots.
2. Pour the oil into a heavy saucepan (medium temp) and toss in the onions.
3. Cook and stir the onions until translucent (5 min.) then add celery and carrots. Sauté them and often stir (3 min.).
4. Add the turkey with a dash of pepper and salt. While cooking, break the meat apart and cook till its red color is gone.
5. Add milk and let it gently simmer. Stir frequently until the milk has completely bubbled away; then mix in the nutmeg.
6. Add wine and let it simmer until it's thoroughly evaporated, then stir in the plum tomatoes.
7. Once tomatoes come to a gentle bubble, lower the heat, and simmer the sauce, uncovered (3 hr.).
8. Occasionally check if you need to add a little liquid to the sauce (about ½ cup of liquid - water or some of the tomato water from your plum tomato can).
9. Taste the Bolognese sauce and season to your liking.
10. Toss with your favorite cooked and drained pasta with a side of parmesan.

Chapter 7: Mediterranean Lean Pork & Lamb Specialties

Pork Favorites

Honey Lemon Pork Chops

Servings Provided: 4

Preparation & Cooking Time: 4 hours 20 minutes (includes marinating time)

What You Need
- Pork rib chops (4)
- Honey (2 tbsp.)
- Lemon peel (2 tbsp.)
- Freshly clipped mint (1 tbsp.)
- Cayenne pepper (.25 tsp.)
- Salt (.5 tsp.)
- Lemon juice (2 tbsp.)
- Olive oil (1 tbsp.)

How To Prepare
1. Chop the mint and shred the lemon peel.
2. Trim the fat from the chops and slice them into one-inch-thick cubes – tossing them into a big zipper-top plastic bag.
3. Whisk the rest of the ingredients and dump it over the pork. Seal the bag.
4. Spin the bag a few times as it marinates (4 hr.).
5. When ready to cook, prepare the grill by greasing the rack with oil. Preheat it with a medium-temperature setting.

6. Arrange the chops on the rack to grill (5 to 6 min. per side). The meat thermometer should reach 160° Fahrenheit or 71° Celsius to serve.

Pork Tenderloin & Couscous - Slow Cooked

Servings Provided: 4

Preparation & Cooking Time: 2 hours 25-30 minutes

What You Need

- Garlic - divided (4 minced cloves)
- Chicken broth (1 cup)
- Pork tenderloins - trimmed (2 @ 12-16 oz./340-450 g each)
- Garam masala (1 tbsp.)
- Salt & pepper (.5 tsp. each)
- Couscous (1 cup)
- Olive oil - EVOO (.5 cup)
- Raisins (.5 cup)
- Toasted - sliced almonds (.5 cup)
- Minced parsley (.5 cup)
- Red wine vinegar (2 tbsp.)

How To Prepare

1. Combine garlic (2 tsp.) and the broth in the slow cooker.
2. Mix the garam masala with the pepper and salt. Use this mixture to rub the tenderloins.
3. Add them to the cooker (side-by-side). Cover and cook 1-2 hours on the low setting or until the meat reaches 145° Fahrenheit/63° Celsius (internal temp). When done, just place on a carving board and cover with foil (tent fashion).
4. Dump the liquid from the cooker, reserving one cup. Add it back to the cooker along with the raisins and couscous. Cover and cook on the high setting about 15 minutes. Fluff and stir in the almonds.
5. Process the vinaigrette by whisking the oil with vinegar, parsley, and rest of the garlic in a mixing container. Season with more pepper and salt to your liking.
6. Slice the tenderloins and serve with the dressed-out vinaigrette couscous!

Roasted Balsamic Pork Loin

Servings Provided: 8

Preparation & Cooking Time: 1 hour 15 minutes + marinating of 2 hours

What You Need

- Steak seasoning rub (2 tbsp.)
- Balsamic vinegar (.5 cup)
- Olive oil (.5 cup)
- Boneless pork loin roast (2 lb./910 g)
- Also Needed: Glass baking dish

How To Prepare

1. Whisk and dissolve the vinegar, steak seasoning, and oil.
2. Toss the pork into a zipper-type bag with the marinade. Tightly squeeze the bag - removing the air, seal, and marinate overnight or at least two hours.
3. Preheat the oven at 350° Fahrenheit or 177° Celsius.
4. Arrange the pork in the baking dish. Bake for one hour or until the internal temp reaches 145° Fahrenheit or 63° Celsius.
5. Transfer the meat to the cutting board and wait for about ten minutes before slicing it to serve.

Rosemary Pork Loin Chops

Servings Provided: 4

Preparation & Cooking Time: 35-40 minutes

What You Need
- Pork loin chops – bone-in or out (4 @ ½-inch thickness)
- Salt and black pepper (.25 tsp. each)
- Dried rosemary (1 tsp.) or fresh (1 tbsp.)
- Garlic (1.5 tsp.)

How To Prepare
1. Heat the oven at 425° Fahrenheit or 218° Celsius to preheat.
2. Dust the chops with pepper and salt. Mince the garlic and whisk it with the rosemary - rub the mix over the chops.
3. Prep a roasting pan using a sheet of foil. Add the chops and adjust the temperature setting to 350° Fahrenheit or 177° Celsius to roast (25 min.), then serve.

Lamb Favorites

Balsamic Lamb Chops

Servings Provided: 4 – 2 chops each

Preparation & Cooking Time: 25-30 minutes

What You Need

- Trimmed lamb rib chops (8 - 4 oz./110 g)
- Lemon (1 juiced & zested)
- Kosher salt (1 tbsp.)
- Olive oil – split (4 tsp.)
- Black pepper (.5 tsp.)
- Balsamic vinegar (3 tbsp.)

How To Prepare

1. Mix one tablespoon of oil with the rind and juice into a Ziploc type bag. Add the chops and coat well. Marinate at room temperature ten minutes.
2. Remove it from the bag and dust with salt and a bit of pepper.
3. Using a med-high temperature setting; lightly spray a pan with a mist of cooking oil spray. Add the lamb and cook two minutes per side until it's the way you like it.
4. Using a saucepan, pour in the vinegar (med-high) and cook until it's syrupy or about three minutes.
5. Drizzle the vinegar and rest of oil (1 teaspoon) over the lamb.
6. Serve with your favorite sides.

Grilled Lamb Chops & Mint

Servings Provided: 6

Preparation & Cooking Time: 15 minutes

What You Need

- Chopped mint leaves (.5 cup + more for garnish)
- Olive oil (.33 cup)
- Sea salt
- Red pepper flakes (.25 tsp.)
- Garlic (2 smashed cloves)
- Rib lamb chops (12 small or 2 1/3 lb.)

How To Prepare

1. Heat the grill to the med-hi setting.
2. Blend the red pepper flakes, olive oil, salt, and mint in a mixing container.
3. Use the garlic to rub the chops.
4. Add a few tablespoons of the mint in a container to cover the lamb. Grill the chops until charred (3-4 min per side).
5. Put the chops on a serving dish and brush with the remainder of the mint oil mixture. Garnish with some bits of mint to serve.

Grilled Lamb Chops With Tomato-Mint Quinoa

Servings Provided: 6-8

Preparation & Cooking Time: 18-20 minutes

What You Need

- Garlic paste or finely minced garlic (1 tsp.)
- Allspice (1 tsp.)
- Sweet paprika (.25 tsp.)
- Black pepper (Scant 1 tsp.)
- Salt (.5 tsp.)
- Ground green cardamom & nutmeg (.5 tsp. each)
- Fresh mint leaves (1 tbsp.)
- Olive oil
- Frenched lamb - separated into chops (2 racks/about 16 chops)
- Lemon (1 large - juiced)
- Yellow or red onion (1 small)

    The Quinoa:

- Dry quinoa (1 cup)
- Water
- Olive oil (2 tbsp.)
- Garlic cloves (3)
- Petit tomato - diced (14.5 oz./410 g can)
- Salt & pepper
- Fresh mint leaves (1 cup + more to garnish)
- Red onion (.5 cup)
- Crumbled feta cheese (.33 or 1/3 cup)

How To Prepare

1. Finely mince the garlic for paste. Combine the garlic and spices with the mint leaves (1 tbsp.) and oil (2 tbsp.). This makes a rub for the lamb.
2. Trim the lamb of its fat and slice the onion. Rinse the quinoa and chop the cloves of garlic. Chop the onion and mint.

3. Rub the lamb chops with the garlic-spice rub. Arrange the chops in a deep dish with oil (2 tbsp.), lemon juice, and onions. Cover and marinate it in the fridge (1-4 hr.).
4. At cooking time, place the chops on the countertop to become room temp (20-25 min.)
5. Prepare the quinoa per its package directions, adding a dash of salt and olive oil to the cooking water (3 cups). Once boiling, lower the heat and add a top. Simmer till the water is gone (15-20 min.).
6. Warm oil (2 tbsp.) in a non-stick pan using a medium temperature setting. Stir in garlic and cook very briefly - then add the canned diced tomato, pepper, and salt. Simmer, stirring intermittently (4-6 min.)
7. Now, stir in the cooked quinoa. Once heated, add the fresh mint. Stir to combine and remove from heat. Now, add the prepared red onions, feta cheese, and additional fresh mint to garnish
8. Time to grill the lamb chops! Warm a grill using high heat. When heated, add the lamb chops and grill (2 min.). Flip the chops over and cook till it's medium-rare (3 min. @ 125° Fahrenheit/52° Celsius) or 3½ minutes @ 135° Fahrenheit/57° Celsius for medium.
9. Let the chops rest for ten minutes before serving.

Lamb Chops With Rosemary & Thyme

Servings Provided: 4

Preparation & Cooking Time: 15 minutes

What You Need
- Lamb loin chops (8 @ 3 oz. @ 85 g each)
- Salt (.25 tsp.)
- Pepper (.5 tsp.)
- Dijon mustard (3 tbsp.)
- Garlic (3 cloves)
- Fresh thyme & rosemary (1 tbsp. each)

How To Prepare
1. Mince the thyme and garlic.
2. Combine the mustard, garlic, rosemary, and thyme in a mixing container. Sprinkle the lamb chops with pepper and salt.
3. Lightly grease the grill rack. Prepare the chops on the grill using the medium-temperature setting (6-8 min.).
4. For Doneness: Med-well is 145° Fahrenheit/63° Celsius; medium is 140° Fahrenheit/60° Celsius.
5. Serve when they are as desired.

Lamb Lettuce Wraps

Servings Provided: 4

Preparation & Cooking Time: 15-20 minutes

What You Need

- Lean ground lamb (6 oz. or 170 g)
- Onion (1 cup)
- Canola oil (2 tsp.)
- Garlic (2 tsp.)
- Cinnamon (1 tsp.)
- Kosher salt (.75 tsp.)
- Black pepper (.25 tsp.)
- Fresh parsley (.5 cup)
- Cucumber (.5 cup)
- Tomato (.5 cup)
- Greek yogurt – plain & fat-free (.25 cup)
- Red pepper hummus (.25 cup)
- Lettuce leaves (8)
- Toasted pine nuts (1 tbsp.)
- Mint leaves (2 tbsp. - torn)

How To Prepare

1. Warm the oil in a skillet using a high-temperature setting on the stovetop. Finely chop and toss in the onions, garlic, salt, cinnamon, and pepper along with the lamb. Sauté until done, or about five minutes.
2. Chop and mix in the cucumber, tomato, and parsley in a mixing container. Stir in the lamb mixture. Mix the hummus and yogurt in another dish.
3. Arrange about ¼ of the lamb fixings in each of the lettuce leaves.
4. Top each one off with a tablespoon of the hummus mixture and garnish.

Mediterranean Lamb Bowls

Servings Provided: 4

Preparation & Cooking Time: 35 minutes

What You Need

The Lamb:
- Ground lamb (1 lb. or 450 g)
- Olive oil (1 tbsp.)
- Garlic cloves (4)
- Onion (.25 cup)
- Ground ginger (.25 tsp.)
- Allspice & paprika (1 tsp. each)
- Red pepper flakes (.5 tsp.)
- Salt and black pepper (as desired)
- Fresh mint (.25 cup + more to garnish)
- Flat-leaf parsley (.25 cup + more to garnish)

The Bowls:
- Turmeric/another preferred rice choice (1 cup)
- Spiced ground lamb (above)
- Tomato (1)
- Cucumber (1)
- Hummus – your choice (1 cup)
- Feta cheese (1 cup)
- Optional to Serve: 2 pita bread

How To Prepare

1. First, finely dice the garlic and onion. Warm a big sauté pan using a medium temperature setting to heat the oil.
2. Once the oil is heated, toss in the garlic and onions to sauté until they're softened (5 min.).
3. Mix in the lamb and cook till done.
4. Then, mix in the ginger, allspice, paprika, red pepper flakes, pepper, and salt till thoroughly incorporated (1-2 min.).

5. Transfer the pan to the countertop and mix in the fresh herbs. Peel and dice the cucumber and tomato.
6. Load a mixing bowl with the turmeric rice, a layer of ground lamb, tomatoes, cucumbers, hummus, and feta.
7. Chop and garnish as desired using a bit more mint and parsley.

Mediterranean Lamb Nachos

Servings Provided: 4

Preparation & Cooking Time: 30 minutes

What You Need
- Garlic (1 clove)
- Tomato (.5 cup)
- Red onion (half of 1)
- Kalamata olives (.25 cup)
- Pita bread (3 pieces)
- Ground lamb (.5 lb./230 g)
- Olive oil (1 tbsp.)
- Coriander (.25 tsp.)
- Cumin (.5 tsp.)
- Black pepper (.5 tsp.)
- Oregano (.25 tsp.)
- Salt (.25 tsp.)
- Feta cheese (2 oz./56 g)
- Cucumber (.33 cup)
- The Topping: Greek yogurt & hummus

How To Prepare
1. Split and slice each pita into eight triangles.
2. Chop the onion, garlic, tomato, and olives.

3. Set the oven temperature setting to 375° Fahrenheit/191° Celsius.
4. Brush olive oil over the triangles and arrange them on a baking tray with pepper and salt.
5. Set a timer to bake the chips for eight to ten minutes until as you like them or golden.
6. Use the medium-temperature setting to warm the oil in a skillet. Pour the oil and sauté the garlic and onion (5 min.).
7. Fold in the lamb, salt, pepper, oregano, cumin, and coriander. Simmer until the pink is gone.
8. Toss the chips into a nacho form and crumble the feta between layers and on top.
9. Broil to melt the cheese and top with the lamb, tomato, cucumber, and olives.
10. Garnish as desired and serve.

Roasted Leg of Lamb With Potatoes

Servings Provided: 8

Preparation & Cooking Time: 2 hours 25 minutes

What You Need

- Leg of lamb - bone-in (4-5 lb./1.8-2.3 kg.)
- Black pepper & salt
- Greek olive oil
- Garlic (5 cloves – as desired)
- Water (2 cups)
- Gold potatoes (8)
- Yellow onion (1)
- Paprika (1 tsp. or to taste)
- Garlic powder (1 tsp.)
- Optional to Garnish: Fresh parsley

  The Rub:
- Paprika (1 tbsp.)
- Ground nutmeg (.5 tbsp.)
- Dried oregano (2 tbsp.)
- Garlic (15 cloves)
- Dried mint flakes (2 tbsp.)
- Olive oil (.5 cup)
- Lemons (2 juiced)

How To Prepare

1. Trim the lamb to remove all fat and place it on the countertop about an hour before prep time, so it's at room temp.
2. Peel and slice the garlic. Peel the onion and potatoes and slice into wedges.
3. Load a food processor to prepare the rub - blending till smooth.
4. At cooking time, dab the meat dry and cut several slits over all sides of the meat and dust with pepper and salt.

5. Set the oven temperature to broil and arrange the leg of lamb on a wire rack and place the rack *directly* on the top oven rack (closest to the broiler element).
6. Broil till the leg portion is seared (5-7 min. per side).
7. Transfer the pan to the countertop and set the oven temperature to 325° Fahrenheit/163° Celsius.
8. Transfer the meat to the countertop and add garlic into the slits.
9. Coat all sides of the lamb with the wet rub and put it in a roasting pan on an inside rack with two cups of water.
10. Dust the potato and onion wedges with garlic powder, paprika, and salt, then add them to the pan.
11. Tent a big sheet of foil over the roasting pan (not touching the lamb) then place the pan on the centermost rack of the oven.
12. Roast covered for about one hour. Discard the foil and continue roasting till the lamb's internal temp is at 130° Fahrenheit/54° Celsius for medium-rare (10-15 min.).
13. Place the lamb on the table and wait about 15 minutes. Then serve the potatoes and lamb with a sprinkle of parsley.

Chapter 8: Mediterranean Lean Beef Specialties

Beef & Couscous Favorite

Servings Provided: 4

Preparation & Cooking Time: 35-40 minutes

What You Need
- Israeli (pearl) couscous (.75 cup)
- Beef flank steak (1 lb. or 450 g)
- Salt-free lemon pepper marinade (5 tbsp.)
- Medium red/yellow tomatoes (2)
- Reduced-fat feta cheese (1 oz. or .25 cup)
- Black pepper (as desired)
- Salt (.125 or 1/8 tsp.)

How To Prepare
1. Discard the seeds and coarsely chop the tomatoes. Crumble the feta.
2. Warm a saucepan using the med-low temperature setting.
3. Dump the couscous into the heated pan and toast for eight to ten minutes, often stirring until it's golden brown. Put it into a mixing container and set it to the side for now.
4. Warm the broiler. Spritz a broiler pan rack with a spritz of cooking oil spray. Pour one tablespoon of the marinade in a custard cup, setting the rest to the side.
5. Brush the beef with the sauce, place it on a rack (4-5 inches from the heat), and cook until done (12-14 min. for medium).
6. Prepare the same saucepan with one cup of water, pepper, and salt. Wait for it to boil, stir in the couscous, and lower the temperature setting.
7. Simmer for seven minutes and pour in the rest of the marinade (4 tbsp.), two tablespoons of feta, and cook until the mix is tender.
8. Serve with the thinly sliced beef and couscous mixture. Garnish it with the rest of the feta (2 tbsp.).

Beef Kofta

Servings Provided: 4

Preparation & Cooking Time: 25 minutes

What You Need
- Ground beef (minimum of 93% lean (1 lb. or 450 g)
- Onions (.5 cup)
- Olive oil (1 tbsp.)
- Ground cinnamon (.25 tsp.)
- Allspice (.25 tsp.)
- Ground cumin & coriander (.5 tsp. each)
- Salt (.5 tsp.)
- Dried mint leaves (.25 tsp.)

How To Prepare
1. Mince the onions.
2. Combine the beef with the onions, oil, cumin, cinnamon, salt, allspice, coriander, and mint leaves in a big mixing container.
3. Shape ¼ of the mixture around eight-inch bamboo skewers leaving roughly one to two inches at the end of the skewer.
4. Make small indentations in the beef mixture with your fingers approximately one inch apart along with the kofta.
5. Continue the process with the rest of the mixture and three skewers.
6. Refrigerate the beef for at least ten minutes.
7. Place the koftas in the middle of the grid over medium, ash-covered coals.
8. Grill with the lid off until the internal temp reaches 160° Fahrenheit/71° Celsius, intermittently turning (12 to 14 min.).

Beef Pitas

Servings Provided: 4

Preparation & Cooking Time: 12-15 minutes

What You Need

- Lean ground beef (1 lb. or 450 g)
- Kosher salt (.5 tsp.)
- Oregano - dried (1 tsp.)
- Black pepper (.25 tsp.)
- Olive oil (1 tbsp.)
- Pocketless pitas (4)
- Hummus (as desired)
- Small red onion (4 slices)
- Fresh flat-leaf parsley (1 tbsp.)
- Lemon wedges

How To Prepare

1. Prepare the beef into sixteen ½-inch thick patties. Dust them with salt, pepper, and oregano.
2. Pour the olive oil into a skillet and heat using the medium-temperature setting. When heated, add the patties, and cook them for two minutes per side (medium).
3. Top the pitas with the hummus, onion, patties, and parsley,
4. Drizzle with the remainder of the oil and serve with the wedges of lemon.

Beef Steaks Crusted in Cumin With Olive-Orange Relish

Servings Provided: 4

Preparation & Cooking Time: 20-25 minutes

What You Need

- Lean steaks (2 - .75-inch - 8-oz. – 230 g)
- Medium oranges (1 to 3)
- Salt (1 tsp.)
- Ground cumin (1.5 tsp.)
- Black pepper (.5 tsp.)
- Red diced onion (.33 or 1/3 cup)
- Kalamata olives (.33 cup)

How To Prepare

1. Heat a big skillet or grill pan using the medium heat setting.
2. Grate two teaspoons orange peel from the oranges and set the oranges to the side. Peel, section, and chop 1-½ cups of the oranges. Coarsely chop the olives.
3. Mix the salt, cumin, and orange peel into a small dish. Save two teaspoons as a seasoning for relish. Combine the pepper to the seasoning and place on each of the steaks.
4. Put the steaks in the prepared skillet and cook for 9-12 minutes, turning twice.
5. Blend the roasted peppers, oranges, onions, and reserved seasonings in a medium dish. Mix well and serve with the relish.

Grilled Beef Lettuce Wraps With Garlic-Yogurt Sauce

Servings Provided: 2

Preparation & Cooking Time: 25 minutes

What You Need

The Sauce:
- Greek yogurt (.75 cup)
- Garlic (2 cloves)
- Fresh lemon juice (2 tsp.)
- Salt (.5 tsp./as desired)
- Fresh dill (1 tsp.) or Dried (.25 tsp.)
- Black pepper (.25 tsp.)

The Wraps:
- Ground beef (1 lb. or 450 g)
- Onion grated (1 small)
- Feta cheese crumbled (4 oz. or 110 g)
- Garlic (3 cloves)
- Fresh parsley (1 tbsp.)
- Oregano - dried (2 tsp.)
- Mint (2 tsp.)
- Pepper & kosher salt (1 tsp. of each)
- For Serving: Large lettuce (8 leaves)

How To Prepare

1. Mince the garlic. Chop the dill, parsley, and mint.
2. Make the sauce by combining each of the fixings in a mixing container. Taste to adjust the pepper and salt as desired. Place the sauce to the side for now.
3. Combine the beef and the rest of the fixings (omit the lettuce) in a mixing container. Prepare eight oval patties and pop them in the fridge until ready to use.
4. Warm a grill using the med-high temperature setting. Grill the patties for three to four minutes per side (150° Fahrenheit/66° Celsius - internal temp).
5. Arrange the patties on a leaf and drizzle them with the sauce. You can also serve the sauce on the side if desired.

Chapter 9: Side Dishes & Vegetables

Pasta Dishes

Broccoli Pasta With White Beans

Servings Provided: 6

Preparation & Cooking Time: 30 minutes

What You Need

- Elbow macaroni - whole wheat (.75 lb./340 g)
- Olive oil - EVOO (.25 cup)
- Red onion (1 small)
- Garlic (6-8 cloves)
- Dried oregano (.5 tsp.)
- Aleppo pepper (.5 tsp.)
- Crushed red pepper - adds a spicy kick (.25 tsp.)
- Frozen broccoli florets (1 lb./450 g - thawed)
- Cannellini beans (15 oz./430 g can)
- Pepper & salt
- Fresh parsley leaves (2 cups)
- Za'atar spice blend (1.5 tsp. + more as desired)
- Grated parmesan cheese (.33 or 1/3 cup)
- Toasted pine nuts (.33 cup)

How To Prepare
1. Cook pasta in salted boiling water (with a splash of oil) according to its packaging instructions till it's al dente.
2. Before you drain pasta, set aside one cup of the pasta cooking water.
3. Meanwhile, finely chop/mince the garlic and onions. Drain and rinse the beans.

4. Prepare a big pot the heat the rest of the oil (med-hi heat) till it's shimmering - not smoking. Toss in the onions and sauté (2 min.) stirring often till they're translucent. Now mix in the garlic, Aleppo pepper, oregano, and crushed pepper flakes.
5. Now, mix in the broccoli florets (thawed) and simmer for four minutes, tossing regularly. Stir in the cannellini beans with pepper and salt to cook (3 min.).
6. Add the cooked pasta and about one-third cup of the reserved cooking water into the pot. Chop and toss in the parsley, za'atar spice, and parmesan cheese - adding a little bit more of the pasta cooking water if needed. Taste and adjust seasoning and simmer till it's heated.
7. Serve with a sprinkle of nuts, more za'atar spice, and additional pepper flakes over the top to serve.

Cannellini Pasta

Servings Provided: 5

Preparation & Cooking Time: 20 minutes

What You Need
- Cannellini beans (15 oz. or 430 g can)
- Bell pepper – red (half of 1)
- Dry penne pasta (2 cups)
- Baby tomatoes (1 cup)
- Garlic (.5 tsp.)
- Onion (half of 1)
- Pasta sauce (2 cups)
- Pure water (.5 cup)
- Dried oregano (.5 tsp.)
- Optional: Mint leaves

How To Prepare
1. Rinse and drain the beans in a colander.
2. Slice the onion and bell pepper. Mince the garlic. Prepare the pasta until it's al dente (8 min.) and drain it.
3. Spritz a skillet using olive oil spray and warm it over a med-high temperature setting. Toss in the garlic to sauté till it's lightly browned.

4. At that point, mix in the rest of the components and wait for them to boil.
5. Once it's tender, add in the pasta.
6. Serve with the feta and mint leaves if desired.

Linguine & Scallops

Servings Provided: 4

Preparation & Cooking Time: 35 minutes

What You Need
- Olive oil (as needed)
- Linguine (12 oz. or 340 g)
- Cherry tomatoes (1 lb. or 450 g)
- Garlic (2 cloves)
- Greek herb blend (1 tsp.)
- Green olives (12)
- Capers (1 tbsp.)
- Sea scallops (1 lb./450 g)
- Fresh cilantro (as desired)

How To Prepare
1. Drain the capers in a colander. Prepare the linguine per the carton instructions. Drain them into a colander.
2. Next, slice the tomatoes into quarters or halves. Mince the garlic and olives.
3. Prepare a large skillet using the medium-temperature setting. Add a thin layer of olive oil and warm until shimmering and add the tomatoes. Simmer until the tomatoes are softened.
4. Mix in the olives, garlic, Greek herbs, and capers to make the sauce rich and tomatoey. Add the pasta and toss with the sauce.
5. In another skillet, warm a tablespoon of oil (med-high temp) till it's shimmering.

6. Remove the side mussels from the scallops and dab them dry using several paper towels. Add them to the pan. Let the scallops cook on one side until they begin to brown. Flip them over and sear the other side.
7. Transfer the scallops to the pasta. Mince and garnish using the cilantro and serve.

Mediterranean Shrimp Penne

Servings Provided: 8

Preparation & Cooking Time: 30 to 35 minutes

What You Need

- Penne pasta (16 oz. or 450 g pkg.)
- Salt (.25 tsp.)
- Olive oil (2 tbsp.)
- Red onion (.25 cup)
- Garlic (1 tbsp.)
- White wine (.25 cup)
- Diced tomatoes (2 cans @ 14.5 oz. or 420 g)
- Shrimp (1 lb.)
- Grated parmesan cheese (1 cup)

How To Prepare

1. Peel and devein the shrimp. Dice the red onion and garlic.
2. Add salt to a big pot of water. Place on the stovetop and set to boil. Toss the pasta in the pot to simmer for nine to ten minutes. Drain.
3. Empty the oil into a skillet. Heat it using the medium heat setting.
4. Mince and add the onion and garlic. Sauté them till tender and pour in the tomatoes and wine. Continue cooking for about ten minutes, occasionally stirring.
5. Fold in the shrimp to cook until it's opaque (5 min.).
6. Combine the pasta and shrimp together and top it off with the cheese to serve.

Rigatoni With Asiago Cheese & Green Olive-Almond Pesto

Servings Provided: 6

Preparation & Cooking Time: 25 minutes

What You Need

- Fresh flat-leaf parsley leaves (.5 cup)
- Green olives 6 oz. or 1.25 cups)
- Uncooked rigatoni (1 lb. or 450 g)
- Water (2 tbsp.)
- Sliced toasted almonds (.5 cup)
- Grated Asiago cheese (.5 cup or 2 oz. approx.)
- White wine vinegar (1 tsp.)
- Garlic (1 large clove)
- Black pepper (.25 tsp.)

How To Prepare

1. Make the rigatoni using the package instructions (omit the fat and salt) and drain. Reserve six tablespoons of the liquid.
2. Load a food processor with the sliced almonds, olives, parsley leaves, garlic, and black pepper. Pulse the ingredients until they hold a coarsely chopped consistency (pulse three times).
3. Leave the processor on and add the vinegar and two tablespoons of water; pulse until the ingredients are finely chopped.
4. Mix the olive combination and ¼ cup of the reserved liquids, as well as the pasta, in a large mixing dish, tossing well.
5. Only add enough of the remainder of the liquid to make the pasta maintain its moist consistency.
6. Sprinkle with the cheese and serve.

Shrimp & Angel Hair Pasta

Servings Provided: 4

Preparation & Cooking Time: 20 minutes

What You Need

- Medium shrimp (1 lb. or 450 g)
- Olive oil (2 tsp.)
- Plum tomatoes (2 cups)
- Garlic (2 cloves)
- Fresh basil (.25 cup)
- Drained capers (2 tbsp.)
- Kalamata olives (.33 or 1/3 cup)
- Black pepper (.25 tsp.)
- Feta cheese (2 oz./.25 cup)
- Cooked angel hair pasta (4 cups or uncooked 8-oz./230 g pkg.)

How To Prepare

1. Slice the basil thin, peel and devein the shrimp, chop the tomatoes, and mince the cloves. Pit and chop the olives. Prepare a skillet with cooking spray.
2. Cook the chosen pasta following the package instructions.
3. Add the garlic in a big pan with the oil using the med-hi setting. Sauté for 30 seconds.
4. Toss in the shrimp and continue to sauté for another minute.
5. Combine the basil and tomato—lower the heat—simmer for an additional three minutes. Blend in the capers, olives, and pepper.
6. Place the shrimp and pasta in a salad dish to toss. Sprinkle the top with the crumbled cheese.

Vegetarian Lasagna Roll-Ups

Servings Provided: 14 rolls

Preparation & Cooking Time: 1 hour 10 minutes

What You Need

- Zucchini (3-4 large)
- Olive oil - ex. Greek Private Reserve olive oil
- Salt
- Lasagna noodles (1 lb. or 450 g)
- Pasta sauce - preferably a tomato & basil (24-oz. or 680 g jar)
- Water (.5 cup)
- Grated parmesan cheese (as desired)
- Optional Ingredient: Crushed red pepper flakes

    For the Filling:

- Ricotta cheese - part-skim or fat-free (20 oz. or 570 g)
- Goat cheese (6 oz. or 170 g)
- Shredded mozzarella – part-skim (2 cups – as desired)
- Italian parsley leaves (1 bunch - about 1 cup)
- Garlic (3 tbsp.)
- Salt & pepper
- Olive oil

How To Prepare

1. Do the prep by chopping the garlic. Thinly slice the zucchini (length-wise).
2. Remove the stems from the parsley and chop.
3. Preheat the oven to 450° Fahrenheit/232° Celsius.
4. Now, bake the zucchini. Brush the zucchini all over and lightly dust with salt.
5. Place them onto (1 or 2) oversized baking trays and bake (10-15 min.).
6. When ready, set aside to slightly cool. Now, adjust the oven temp to reach 350° Fahrenheit/177° Celsius.
7. Prepare a pot of water to cook the noodles with salt (12 min. or so).

8. Then, drain them into a colander and add to a container of cold water to halt cooking. Drain and arrange the noodles onto a big flat tray covered with parchment paper.
9. Next prepare the filling by mixing the goat cheese with the ricotta, shredded mozzarella, garlic, chopped parsley, pepper, and salt. Add a bit of oil (no more than 1 tbsp.). Mix thoroughly till the cheese mixture is thoroughly combined.
10. Evenly spread the prepared filling on each of the noodles. Top with a slice of the zucchini, then roll the noodles tightly with the seams downward.
11. Prepare a baking dish (9x13-inch) and add ¾ of the pasta sauce and water (1/2 cup) to the baking dish.
12. Carefully place the rolls on the baking sheet (upright), then top with the rest of the pasta sauce, a dusting of parmesan cheese, and additional shredded mozzarella as desired
13. Bake 40 minutes. Check halfway through and add more liquid as needed (more pasta sauce or water).
14. Remove from heat, garnish with fresh basil leaves, and serve with your favorite side salad and a crusty bread.

Veggie Options

Baked Zucchini Sticks

Servings Provided: 8

Preparation & Cooking Time: 30 minutes

What You Need
- Zucchini (4 medium)
- Kalamata olives (.5 cup)
- Tomatoes (.5 cup)
- Garlic (3 large cloves)
- Dried oregano (1 tbsp.)
- Black pepper (.25 tsp.)
- Feta cheese (.25 cup)
- Parsley (.25 cup)

How To Prepare
1. Set the oven temperature to reach 350° Fahrenheit/177° Celsius.
2. Slice the zucchini lengthwise and into halves. Remove the middle and discard the flesh. Finely chop the veggies and mince the cloves.
3. Use a medium dish and add the tomatoes, peppers, garlic, black pepper, and oregano.
4. Spread the mixture into the zucchini and arrange on a baking dish. Bake 15 minutes and top with the feta. Bake another three minutes until the cheese has browned.
5. Serve hot or cold with a sprinkle of parsley.

Chickpea Cauliflower Couscous

Servings Provided: 6

Preparation & Cooking Time: 30-35 minutes

What You Need

- Butter (2 tbsp.)
- Olive oil (2 tbsp.)
- Dried apricots (.5 cup)
- Head of cauliflower (3 lb./1 large/8 cups)
- Garlic (2 cloves)
- Onion (1 medium)
- Fresh baby spinach (2.5 cups/2.5 oz./70 g)
- Chickpeas/garbanzo beans (15 oz./430 g can)
- Roasted pistachios or toasted walnuts (.5 cup - chopped)
- Salt (.5 tsp.)
- Sliced green onions (.5 cup)

How To Prepare

1. Rinse and drain the beans. Snip the dried apricots and cover them with boiling water in a small bowl. Wait about ten minutes for them to plump. Drain thoroughly.
2. Prepare the cauliflower in batches using the food processor.
3. Prep the skillet using one tablespoon each of oil and butter over the med-high temperature setting.
4. Slice the onion and sauté it for three minutes until it starts browning.
5. Mince and toss the garlic and sauté them for another ½ minute.
6. Prep the cauliflower into florets and add them in an even layer.
7. Sauté them for eight minutes until the mix is golden.
8. Even the layers. Chop the spinach and slice the green onions.
9. Add in the salt, pistachios, chickpeas, spinach, and drained apricots. Stir well and add the butter and green onions, thoroughly tossing until the butter has melted.
10. Serve with the remainder of the oil.

Fasolakia Lathera - Greek Green Beans

Servings Provided: 2 main or 4 side dishes

Preparation & Cooking Time: 50 minutes

What You Need

- Olive oil (.33 cup)
- Onion (1)
- Green beans (1 lb. or 450 g)
- Potato sliced (1 medium)
- Medium tomatoes (3 grated) or Chopped tomatoes (12-15 oz. or 340-430 g)
- Chopped parsley (.25 cup)
- Sugar (1 tsp.)
- Salt & pepper (.5 tsp/as desired)

How To Prepare

1. In a medium pot, warm the oil using the med-low temperature setting. Chop and sauté the onion until softened.
2. Cut the potato into a ¼-inch thickness and cut it in half. Toss in the potatoes and continue cooking for two to three minutes. Mix in the beans, tomatoes, parsley, sugar, pepper, and salt. Mix and add in just enough water to cover the beans.
3. Simmer – don't boil - with the top on (40 min.).
4. The beans are ready once there is no water left and the beans are soft.
5. Enjoy the vegan-friendly dish with bread and feta cheese (if desired).

Fried Garlicy Tomatoes

Servings Provided: 4

Preparation & Cooking Time: 20 minutes

What You Need

- Vine-ripe tomatoes (2.5 lb. or 4-6 large or 1.1 kg.)
- Olive oil (.25 cup)
- Garlic (10 cloves - not crushed)
- Fresh green/red chilies (2-3)
- Salt (.5 tsp.)
- Fresh mint leaves (1 small bunch) or dried (2 tsp.)

How To Prepare

1. Start by slicing each tomato horizontally in half (through the tip).
2. Place the tomato halves cut-side down in a skillet. Pour the oil over the tomatoes and heat them using medium heat (5 min.).
3. Finely chop the garlic, chiles, and mint.
4. Flip the tomatoes and sprinkle about half the chilies and garlic over the tops - then add the other into the pan.
5. Sprinkle with the salt, put a lid on the pan, lower the temperature - simmer till the tomatoes have started to soften - yet still retain their shape (15 min.).
6. While cooking, tilt the pan several times and scoop some of the oil mixture over the tomatoes. Continue cooking for another minute or two.
7. When almost done, sprinkle the mint over the tomatoes, cover the pan, and continue cooking (1-2 min.).
8. Remove the pan from the burner and serve.

Grilled Zucchini Boats Loaded With Tomatoes & Feta

Servings Provided: 6

Preparation & Cooking Time: 17-20 minutes

What You Need
- Zucchini (3)
- Olive oil/Greek EVOO (as needed)
- Kosher salt & black pepper (to taste)
- Dried oregano (as desired)
- Cherry tomatoes (6 oz./170 g)
- Green onions both white and green parts (3)
- Crumbled feta cheese (.5 tsp. + more as desired)
- Fresh mint (6-10 leaves)
- Fresh parsley (1 handful)
- Lemon (1 zested)
- Lemon juice (1 splash)
- Suggestion: Cast-iron skillet or indoor griddle

How To Prepare
1. Warm a skillet/griddle using a medium-temperature setting. (OR, If cooking on a gas grill, lightly oil the grate and preheat the grill to med-low).
2. Rinse the zucchini and trim it by slicing it lengthwise into halves.
3. Generously brush the zucchini with oil and dust it using salt, pepper, and oregano.
4. Arrange the zucchini on the preheated grill (or indoor griddle) with the flesh-side down. Grill until soft and nicely charred (3-5 min.). Flip the fish over and grill for another three to five minutes until this side is also tender and gains some color. (For an indoor skillet/griddle, you might need to adjust the temperature setting to med-high.)
5. Transfer the pan of zucchini from the burner to cool for easy handling.
6. Use a small spoon to scoop the flesh (don't discard). Squeeze the liquids from the zucchini flesh using a paper towel or kitchen linen towel.
7. Make the filling for the zucchini boats. Chop the mint and parsley.
8. Slice the tomatoes into halves.

9. Put the zucchini flesh in a mixing bowl. Trim the ends and chop the onions.
10. Add the tomatoes, feta, onions, parsley, mint, and lemon zest.
11. Mix in a small splash of lemon juice and sprinkle of oregano.
12. Drizzle oil over them and thoroughly toss.
13. Scoop mixture into the boats and serve.
14. You will have 51 calories with 1.9 total fats and 4.3 net carbs.

Loaded Portobello Burger

Servings Provided: 4

Preparation & Cooking Time: 25 minutes

What You Need
- Garlic (1 clove)
- Tomato (.5 cup)
- Portobello mushroom caps (4)
- Olive oil (2 tbsp)
- Sea salt (.5 tsp.)
- Country-style whole wheat bread (4 slices)
- Jarred roasted red peppers (.5 cup)
- Pitted Kalamata olives (2 tbsp.)
- Mixed baby salad greens (16 oz./450 g or 2 cups)
- Dried oregano (.5 tsp.)
- Red wine vinegar (1 tbsp.)
- Crumbled reduced-fat feta cheese (.25 cup)
- Optional: Egg (as desired)

How To Prepare
1. Do the prep by chopping the olives and tomatoes. Mince the garlic and slice the red peppers. Remove the gills and stems from the mushrooms.
2. Set the grill at medium-high.
3. Use a butter knife to mash the garlic and sea salt on a cutting block into a smooth paste. Mix it with the oil and brush it over the mushrooms and one side of the bread.
4. Combine the feta, olives, red peppers, vinegar, tomato, oregano, and one tablespoon of oil in a medium mixing container.
5. Grill them until the caps are tender (4 min. each side). Grill the bread until it's crispy (1 min. each side).
6. Toss the greens with the pepper mixture.
7. Place the mushrooms with the top side facing downward on four slices of bread. Top it off with the salad mix and the rest of the bread.
8. Add a slice of juicy pineapple to serve.

Mediterranean Zucchini Casserole

Servings Provided: 4-6

Preparation & Cooking Time: 1 hour 15 minutes

What You Need

- Olive oil
- Yellow onion (1 halved)
- Garlic cloves (2)
- Ground turkey or beef (1 lb./450 g @ 97% lean)
- Black pepper & salt
- Ground allspice (1.5 tsp.)
- Spanish-style sweet paprika (1 tsp.)
- Ground nutmeg (.5 tsp.)
- Chopped - canned tomatoes with the juice (1.5 cups)
- Tomato paste (2 tbsp.)
- Water (1 cup)
- Zucchini (2-3)
- Carrots (2)
- To Garnish: Generous handful fresh parsley

How To Prepare

1. Warm the oven at 375° Fahrenheit/191° Celsius.
2. Next, warm the oil (2 tbsp.) in a saucepan using a medium temperature setting till heated and shimmering - not smoking.
3. Chop half of the onion and slice the other into rings.
4. Toss in the chopped garlic and onions to sauté, stirring regularly until tender and fragrant (not browned).
5. Add meat with salt and pepper, breaking it apart as it cooks.
6. Raise the temperature to med-high and cook till the meat is thoroughly browned, stirring occasionally. Carefully drain any juices or fat and return the saucepan back to the burner to heat.
7. Mix in the paprika, allspice, and nutmeg. Now mix in the canned, chopped tomatoes with juice, tomato paste, and water.

8. Wait for it to boil, then reduce the temperature to simmer (7-10 min.). Remove from the burner.
9. Slice the carrots and zucchini into thin rounds. Chop the parsley.
10. Add zucchini, carrots, and sliced onions to a casserole dish. Add the meat sauce and spread evenly.
11. Tightly cover the casserole dish with foil and bake (40 min.).
12. Now, uncover, and then broil for a brief few minutes, watching carefully.
13. Remove from oven and garnish with fresh parsley. Transfer to dinner bowls, add a drizzle of oil. Serve with a portion of rice or your favorite crusty bread.

Mushroom Kabobs

Servings Provided: 6

Preparation & Cooking Time: 45-50 minutes

What You'll Need:
- Olive oil (2 tbsp.)
- Cremini mushrooms (1 lb. or 450 g)
- Black pepper (1 dash)
- Balsamic vinegar (.25 cup)
- Oregano (.5 tsp.)
- Basil (.5 tsp.)
- Kosher salt (as desired)
- Freshly chopped parsley leaves (2 tbsp.)
- Garlic cloves (3 minced)

How To Prepare
1. Warm the oven ahead of time to reach 425° Fahrenheit/218° Celsius.
2. Prepare a baking tray using a spritz of oil.
3. Whisk the oil, vinegar, oregano, garlic, and basil in a big mixing container. Combine with a dash salt or pepper, then, add the mushrooms. Let the mixture rest for about 10-15 minutes.
4. Push the mushrooms onto skewers and place on the cooking sheet.
5. Roast approximately 15-20 minutes. Sprinkle with parsley as a garnish.

Red Pepper Pasta With Sweet Potatoes

Servings Provided: 4

Preparation & Cooking Time: 25 minutes

What You Need

- Whole wheat angel hair pasta (1 cup/8 oz./230 g)
- Olive oil (2 tbsp.)
- Garlic cloves (4)
- Peeled-shredded sweet potato (3 cups/1 medium)
- Red bell pepper (1 large)
- Plum tomatoes (1 cup)
- Water (.5 cup)
- Fresh tarragon (1 tbsp.)
- Fresh parsley (2 tbsp.)
- White wine vinegar (1 tbsp.)
- Crumbled goat cheese (.5 cup)
- Sea salt (.75 tsp.)

How To Prepare

1. Prepare a big pot of boiling water. Toss in the pasta to cook till it's al dente (4-5 min.).
2. Pour the oil into the skillet and warm it using a medium-temperature setting.
3. Thinly slice the bell pepper. Mince or dice and add the garlic and tomatoes. Sauté them for about two to five minutes and add the potato, water, and bell peppers. Stir occasionally for five to seven minutes.
4. Transfer the pan to the countertop and cover.
5. Chop the tarragon and parsley.
6. Drain the pasta (saving ½ cup of the liquids).
7. Toss the pasta into the pot with the veggie mixture, parsley, rest of the oil, vinegar, oregano, goat cheese, and sea salt. Stir in the pasta water (2 tbsp. at a time) to reach the favored consistency and serve.

Spanakorizo - Greek Spinach & Rice

Servings Provided: 2

Preparation & Cooking Time: 30 minutes

What You Need

- Fresh spinach rinsed (1 lb./450 g)
- Juice of ½ lemon
- Yellow onion (1) or Spring onions (2-3)
- Olive oil (2.5 tbsp. + more as needed)
- Chopped dill (1-2 tbsp.)
- Dry mint (1 tsp.)
- Water (2/3 cups)
- Rice - medium-grain preferred (1/3 cup or 60 g)
- Salt & pepper
- Tomato paste (1 tbsp./optional)

How To Prepare

1. Prep a big pot to wilt the spinach. Add the oil (1 tsp.) and lemon juice. Once wilted, set it aside to drain.
2. Mince the onion and add it to another pan to sauté the onion with the remainder of the oil until softened.
3. Fold in the spinach, dill, dry mint, salt, pepper, and warm water. Wait for it to boil.
4. Mix in the rice. Simmer it with a lid on until the rice is softened (20 min.). Add warm water as needed.
5. Serve as desired with a spritz of oil and juice of lemon with a portion of feta.

Spinach & Fried Rice With Artichokes & Peppers

Servings Provided: 4

Preparation & Cooking Time: 15-20 minutes

What You Need

- Cooked rice (1.5 cups)
- Frozen spinach (10 oz. or 280 g)
- Minced garlic (.5 tsp.)
- Marinated artichoke hearts (6 oz. or 170 g)
- Roasted red peppers (4 oz. or 110 g)
- Feta cheese with herbs (.5 cup)
- Olive oil (2 tbsp.)

How To Prepare

1. Prepare the vegetables. Mince the garlic. Thaw, drain, and chop the frozen spinach. Drain and quarter the artichoke hearts. Drain and chop the roasted red peppers.
2. Use the medium-temperature setting on the stovetop to warm a frying pan and heat the oil. Toss in the garlic to sauté (2 min.).
3. Toss in the rice and continue cooking until well heated (2 min.).
4. Fold in the spinach and continue cooking for three minutes.
5. Next, add the red peppers and artichoke hearts to simmer for two minutes.
6. Crumble and add feta cheese to serve.

Stuffed Eggplant

Servings Provided: 4

Preparation & Cooking Time: 50 minutes

What You Need
- Garlic (2 cloves)
- Red onion (1)
- Cremini mushrooms (1 pint)
- Medium eggplants (2)
- Cooked quinoa (2 cups)
- Olive oil - divided (3 tbsp.)
- Torn kale (2 cups)
- Freshly chopped thyme (1 tbsp.)
- Juice & zest (1 lemon + lemon wedges to serve)
- Freshly cracked black pepper & salt (as desired)
- Greek yogurt - plain (.5 cup)
- The Garnish: Freshly chopped parsley (3 tbsp.)

How To Prepare
1. Set the oven temperature to reach 400° Fahrenheit/204° Celsius.
2. Cover a baking tray using a sheet of parchment baking paper.
3. Slice the eggplant. Using a spoon, scoop out 1/3 of the flesh inside the eggplants and discard or use it for another recipe.
4. Rub the inside of each eggplant half with oil (1.5 tsp.). Place it onto the baking tray.
5. Pour the remainder of the oil into a big skillet and heat it with a medium-temperature setting.
6. Mince and toss in the onion to sauté until tender (3-4 min.). Also, mince and add the garlic to sauté it until it's fragrant (1 min.).
7. Quarter and fold in the mushrooms. Sauté them until they are just tender (4-5 min.).
8. Mix in the quinoa and kale. Simmer till the kale is slightly wilted (2-3 min.). Mix in the lemon juice and zest, thyme, pepper, and salt.
9. Scoop the filling into the prepared eggplants. Roast until the eggplants are tender - not falling apart (17-20 min.). Cool for five minutes.

10. Promptly serve the eggplant with a garnish of parsley, a portion of yogurt, and lemon wedges if desired.

Zesty Chargrilled Broccolini

Servings Provided: 4

Preparation & Cooking Time: 10 minutes

What You Need
- Broccolini (10.5 oz./300g)
- Avocado oil (as needed)
- Lemon (1)
- Black pepper & Kosher salt (to taste)
- For Serving - as desired: Pumpkin & sunflower seeds

How To Prepare
1. Set a griddle or grill pan over high heat. Spritz it using a drizzle of avocado oil.
2. Toss the broccolini in the pan so that the grill marks will run horizontally.
3. Cook for five minutes, flipping halfway through.
4. Grate the zest from the lemon over the top with a dusting of salt and pepper.
5. Spritz with lemon juice and toss in the sunflower and pumpkin seeds to serve.

Chapter 10: Mediterranean Appetizer & Snack Specialties

Sweet Snacks

Baked Apricots

Servings Provided: 5

Preparation & Cooking Time: 25-30 minutes

What You Need

- Raw cane/brown/regular sugar (3 tbsp.)
- Butter - room temp (2 tbsp.)
- Vanilla extract (.5 tsp.)
- Cinnamon (1 tsp.)
- Apricots (6)

    Optional:
- Vanilla ice cream (6 scoops or to your liking)
- Cinnamon sticks (6)

How To Prepare

1. Wash, dry, and slice the apricots into halves and place them on a baking tray.
2. Set the oven to reach 375° Fahrenheit or 191° Celsius.
3. Mix the butter, sugar, cinnamon, and vanilla (30 seconds to 1 min.) until it is thickened. Scoop it into each of the apricot halves.
4. Bake them for 12 minutes and chill for about ten minutes.
5. Serve two halves with ice cream and a drizzle of syrup.
6. Add a cinnamon stick on the side and serve warm.

Blueberry-Coconut Energy Bites

Servings Provided: 12

Preparation & Cooking Time: 10 minutes

What You Need
- Old-fashioned rolled/gluten-free oats (1 cup)
- Ground flaxseed meal (.25 cup)
- Chia seeds (2 tbsp.)
- Ground cinnamon (.25 tsp.)
- Sea salt (1 dash)
- Creamy almond butter (.5 cup)
- Honey (.25 cup)
- Vanilla extract (.5 tsp.)
- Optional: Coconut extract (.5 tsp.)
- Dried blueberries (.25 cup)
- Sweetened flaked coconut (.25 cup)

How To Prepare
1. Toss the oats with ground flaxseed, chia seeds, cinnamon, and salt.
2. Place the almond butter in a microwave-safe bowl and warm it until slightly melted (20-30 sec.) and stir till it's silky.
3. Stir in the honey, vanilla, and coconut extract to the melted almond butter. Pour over the oat mixture and stir.
4. Now, stir in the dried blueberries and coconut.
5. Roll the mixture into small balls (1-2 tbsp. per ball). Place in a closed container and keep refrigerated for up to two weeks or in the freezer for a month.

Date & Prosciutto Wraps

Servings Provided: 16

Preparation & Cooking Time: 10 minutes

What You Need
- Prosciutto (16 portions)
- Pitted dates (16 whole)
- Black pepper (to your liking)

How To Prepare
1. Thinly slice the prosciutto.
2. Wrap one slice of prosciutto around each of the dates.
3. When done, serve with a bit of freshly cracked black pepper.

Delicious Energy Bites

Servings Provided: 20 balls

Preparation & Cooking Time: 10 minutes

What You Need
- Cashew nuts, raw, unsalted (2 cups)
- Dried apricots (1 cup)
- Shredded unsweetened coconut (.33 or 1/3 cup)
- Chopped dates (.25 cup)
- Zest from 1 orange & lemon (1 tsp. each)
- Cinnamon (.5 tsp.)
- Ground ginger (.5 tsp.)
- Salt (.125 or 1/8 tsp.)

How To Prepare
1. Toss the cashew nuts with the apricots, coconut, and dates in a food processor. Pulse till the mixture is crumbly.

2. Next, mix in the citrus zest, salt, and spices. Pulse using a high speed until the mixture starts to stick together.
3. Cover a tray with parchment baking paper. Shape the mixture into (20) one-inch balls.
4. Store in the fridge in a sealed container (3 days). Or store in the freezer for up to three weeks.

Easy Roasted Fruit

Servings Provided: 4

Preparation & Cooking Time: 30 minutes

What You Need
- Peaches (4)
- Fresh blueberries (1.5 cups)
- Ground cinnamon (.125 or 1/8 tsp.)
- Brown sugar (3 tbsp.)

How To Prepare
1. Set the oven to 350° Fahrenheit/177° Celsius.
2. Peel, slice, and scatter the peaches and blueberries into a baking dish.
3. Sprinkle them using cinnamon and brown sugar.
4. Bake for about 20 minutes, then adjust oven settings to a low-broil until bubbly (5 min.).
5. Serve as desired.

Honey-Almond Peaches

Servings Provided: 4

Preparation & Cooking Time: 20-25 minutes

What You Need

- Peaches (15 oz./425 g can)
- Honey (2 tbsp.)
- Cardamom (.25 tsp.)
- Low-fat ricotta cheese (.5 cup)
- Almonds (.25 cup)

How To Prepare

1. Rinse the peaches and cut into halves. Place on a baking sheet.
2. Combine the cheese with the cardamom and honey. Spoon the fixings into the halves. Bake for 15 minutes at 400° Fahrenheit/204° Celsius.
3. Using a food processor, coarsely ground the almonds, and toast them in a skillet using a medium temperature setting.
4. Sprinkle the nuts over the peaches and serve.

Honey Pistachio Roasted Pears

Servings Provided: 6

Preparation & Cooking Time: 30-35 minutes

What You Need

- Firm medium pears (3 ripe)
- Honey (3 tbsp.)
- Butter (2 tbsp.)
- Pear nectar (.25 cup)
- Grated orange zest (1 tsp.)
- Powdered sugar (2 tbsp.)
- Mascarpone cheese (.5 cup)
- Salted pistachios – roasted & chopped (1/3 cup)
- Also Needed: 2-qt. rectangular baking dish

How To Prepare

1. Set the oven temperature to 400° Fahrenheit/204° Celsius.
2. Peel, core, and cut the pears into halves. Arrange them cut side down in the baking dish.
3. Combine and add the nectar, honey, butter, and zest. Pour it over the pears.
4. Roast with the lid off for 20-25 minutes to serve.

Lemon Bars

Servings Provided: 12

Preparation & Cooking Time: 40 minutes

What You Need

The Crust:
- Melted & cooled butter (.25 cup)
- Pure maple syrup (.25 cup)
- Almond extract (.25 tsp.)
- Fine blanched almond flour - not meal (packed - 1.5 cups)
- Coconut flour (2 tbsp.)
- Salt (.25 tsp.)

The Filling:
- Lemon: Zested (1) & juiced @ .66 or 2/3 cup - from 2-4 lemons)
- Pure maple syrup (.5 cup)
- Eggs (4 large)
- Coconut flour - sifted/arrowroot starch (1 tbsp.)

To Garnish:
- Powdered sugar - sifted
- Zested lemon

Also Needed:
- 8x8-inch or 20x20-cm baking pan (not glass)
- Parchment baking paper

How To Prepare
1. Set the oven temperature at 350° Fahrenheit/177° Celsius.
2. Cover the baking tray with paper.
3. Whisk the almond flour with the salt and coconut flour.
4. Next fold in the maple syrup, butter, and almond extract; mixing to make the dough, then evenly pressing it into the pan to bake (15 min.).
5. Meanwhile, prepare the filling in a mixing container, by thoroughly incorporating the lemon zest with the lemon juice, eggs, maple syrup, and coconut flour.

6. When the crust is ready (and hot), immediately and slowly pour the filling over the crust.
7. Adjust the oven temperature setting to 325° Fahrenheit/163° Celsius, put them in the oven to bake until filling is set and no longer jiggles (20-25 min.).
8. Thoroughly cool on a wire rack - then chill them in the fridge (4 hr.).
9. Once ready, slice, and garnish them with powdered sugar and a portion of lemon zest to serve.

Mediterranean Baked Apples

Servings Provided: 4

Preparation & Cooking Time: 55 minutes

What You Need
- Honey (4 tbsp.)
- Nutmeg (.25 tsp.)
- Allspice (.25 tsp.)
- Ground cinnamon (.5 tsp.)
- Chopped almonds/walnuts (.5 cup)
- Golden raisins (.5 cup)
- Lemon - juice & zest (half of 1)

How To Prepare
1. Set the oven temperature to 350° Fahrenheit/177° Celsius.
2. Core the apples and arrange them in a baking dish.
3. Combine the remainder of the fixings and fill the cores.
4. Use the rest scooped on the top.
5. Pour ½-inch of water into the baking dish. Add the apples and arrange on the middle shelf of the oven. Bake till they're as desired (40-45 min.).
6. Arrange the apples on serving plates. Pour the juices from the baking dish over them and serve.

Pasteli - Greek Honey Sesame Bars

Servings Provided: 20

Preparation & Cooking Time: 10 minutes

What You Need
- Honey (7.5 oz. or 220 g)
- Sesame seeds (7.5 oz.)
- Salt (1 dash)
- Lemon - zested (1 medium)

How To Prepare
1. Toast the sesame seeds. Place a frying pan on a burner using the high-temperature setting. Add the seeds and toast them for two to three minutes until golden - not dark. Remove the sesame seeds from the pan and set them aside. If you prefer, use the oven, set the temperature at 375° Fahrenheit or 191° Celsius and toast the seeds.
2. In the same pan, add the honey and wait for it to foam. Add a pinch of salt and the toasted sesame seeds. Reduce the temperature setting to medium and continuously stir it with a wooden spoon until nicely colored (3-5 min.). Be careful not to burn the mixture.
3. Transfer the pan to a cool burner. Mix in the lemon zest.
4. Line a round pan (22cm/8.5 inches in diameter) with parchment paper and empty in the mixture. Carefully spread the mixture over the paper.
5. Let the pasteli *slightly* cool for about 20 minutes and cut them into 20 portions.

Poached Cherries

Servings Provided: 4-5

Preparation & Cooking Time: 15 minutes

What You Need

- Sugar (.66 or 2/3 cup)
- Water (1.75 cups)
- Lemon & orange zest (3 strips at 1x3-inch or 3x8-cm each)
- Vanilla bean – split (¼ of 1)
- Peppercorns (15)
- Fresh sweet cherries (1 lb. or 450 g)

How To Prepare

1. Rinse and pit the cherries and cut the lemon into strips.
2. Add the water to a saucepan along with the zest, sugar, peppercorns, and vanilla bean.
3. Stir until the sugar dissolves and add the cherries, simmering about ten minutes.
4. Remove any foam and let them cool in the fridge.
5. Strain the liquid and serve.

Popped Quinoa Crunch Bars

Servings Provided: 20 bars

Preparation & Cooking Time: 10 minutes

What You Need

- Semi-sweet chocolate bars - ex. Baker's (4 @ 4 oz./110 g each - 16 oz./450 g total)
- Dry quinoa (1 cup)
- PB2 (1 tbsp.)
- Vanilla (.5 tsp.)

    The Drizzle:

- Water (2 tbsp.)
- PB2 (2.5 tbsp.)

How To Prepare

1. Heat a big, heavy-bottomed pot using a med-high temperature setting.
2. Once heated add the quinoa 1/4 cup at a time (4 batches).
3. Occasionally swirl the mixture till you hear light popping.
4. Swirl about one minute till the popping has subsided slightly. Pour into a holding dish for now.
5. Chop and melt the chocolate in a double boiler and mix it with the PB2, quinoa, and vanilla - stirring till incorporated.
6. Cover a baking tray using a sheet of parchment baking paper - spread the prepared quinoa mixture across a baking sheet (½-inch thickness is good).
7. Smear it over the top of the chocolate-quinoa, and then gently swirl it around using a butter knife.
8. Pop it into the fridge till it's totally firm (1 hr.) before slicing to serve.

Snack Boxes & Trays

All-Green Crudites Basket

Servings Provided: 8

Preparation & Cooking Time: 10 minutes

What You Need

- String beans or haricot verts (8 oz. or 230 g)
- Broccoli (1 head)
- Cucumber (1 medium)
- Fennel (1 bulb)
- Celery (1 bunch)
- Green pepper (1)
- Endive (3 heads - big leaves – sliced vertically into halves)

How To Prepare

1. First, rinse and chop the broccoli into florets. Trim the beans. Core, seed, and slice the green peppers, and slice the fennel into vertical slices. Cut the celery and cucumber into sticks.
2. Prep a big pot of salted water and wait for it to boil. Then, fill a big container with ice water.
3. Dip the beans and broccoli into the water and cook until bright green (1 min.). Drain and scoop them into the ice water bath to thoroughly cool. Dab them dry using paper towels.
4. Place the prepared goods onto a platter. Group them as desired, placed close together to remain upright.

Charcuterie Bistro Lunch Box

Servings Provided: 1

Preparation & Cooking Time: 5 minutes

What You Need
- Mozzarella stick (1 - halved)
- Prosciutto (1 slice)
- Breadsticks (2 halved)
- Grapes (.5 cup)
- Radishes (2 large - halved) or English cucumber (4 slices @ ¼-inch each)
- Dates (2)

How To Prepare
1. Slice the prosciutto in half lengthwise. Next, wrap a slice around each portion of cheese.
2. Arrange the breadsticks, wrapped cheese, dates, grapes, and radishes or cucumber in a four-cup divided sealable container.
3. Keep refrigerated until ready to eat.

Fruit Charcuterie Board

Servings Provided: 12-16

Preparation & Cooking Time: 20 minutes

What You Need

- Blue cheese (4 oz./110 g)
- Aged goat cheese (4 oz.)
- Brie (4 oz.)
- Soft - triple crème cheese (4 oz.)
- Cotswold cheese (4 oz.)
- Kiwis (3)
- Golden kiwis (3)
- Mangoes (2)
- Grapes (4 small bunches)
- Cherries (4 handfuls)
- Figs (8)
- Peaches (2)
- White peaches (2)
- Apricots (3)
- Watermelon (1 cup)
- Plums (3)
- Cantaloupe (1 cup)
- Strawberries (1 cup)
- Raspberries (1 cup)
- Blackberries (1 cup)
- Golden raspberries (1 cup)

How To Prepare

1. Set the rainbow with this tray. Do the prep. Peel and thickly slice the kiwis, peaches, apricots, and plums. Then peel and dice the mangoes, watermelon, and cantaloupe. Slice the strawberries into halves and quarter the figs.
2. Arrange the cheeses on a fancy platter and wait to serve till they're softened (20-30 min.).
3. Arrange the fruit in clusters around the cheese and you're ready!

Rainbow Heirloom Tomato Bruschetta Tray

Servings Provided: 8

Preparation & Cooking Time: 15 minutes

What You Need
- Baguette (1)
- Garlic cloves (3)
- Whole-milk ricotta cheese (16 oz./450 g)
- Black pepper & kosher salt
- Balsamic vinegar (2 tbsp.)
- Basil pesto (.25 cup)
- Olive oil (2 tbsp.)
- Dill sprigs (2 tbsp.)
- Tomatoes (1 each - green - yellow & red)
- Heirloom cherry tomatoes (1 pint)
- To Serve: Fresh basil leaves

How To Prepare
1. Use a party tray to prepare this delicious snack.
2. First, thinly slice and toast the bread. Slice the cherry tomatoes into halves. Halve the garlic cloves, thinly slice the tomatoes, and chop the dill.
3. Rub the surface of each baguette slice with the garlic cloves.
4. Flavor the ricotta with pepper and salt - then spread it over the slices.
5. Whisk the pesto with the oil, balsamic vinegar, and dill. Add the tomatoes and gently toss.
6. Working in color blocks, arrange the tomatoes on the baguette slices with a dusting of pepper and salt. Top with basil leaves.

Tuna Protein Box

Servings Provided: 4

Preparation & Cooking Time: 20 minutes

What You Need

- Whole eggs (4)
- Carrots (4)
- Celery (2-3 ribs)
- Grapes (1 cup)
- Blueberries (1 cup)
- Cheese (8 oz./230 g)

    The Tuna Salad:

- Tuna (5 oz./140 g can)
- Mayonnaise (2 tbsp.)
- Celery (2 tbsp.)
- Pepper & salt (as desired)

How To Prepare

1. Cook and cool hard-boiled eggs. You can leave them with the shells on or peel them after they've cooled completely. Now, peel and chop the carrots and celery. Dice the cheese into cubes. Drain the tuna.
2. Stir together tuna salad ingredients and divide between containers.
3. Divide all other ingredients between containers.
4. Enjoy cold.

Other Snacks

Baked Beet Chips

Servings Provided: 3-4 cups

Preparation & Cooking Time: 25-30 minutes

What You Need

- Olive oil
- Beets (6-8 @ medium-large)
- Dried chives (1 tbsp.)
- Sea salt - flaked (1 tbsp.)

How To Prepare

1. Trim the beets to remove the roots and greens, then thoroughly scrub the beets under cold water, leaving the skins on. Use a sharp knife to slice the beets (1/16-inch thin).
2. Set the oven temperature at 400° Fahrenheit/204° Celsius.
3. Drizzle a tiny bit of oil onto a baking sheet pan - greasing it with a paper towel or your hands (or use a cooking oil spray).
4. Layer the beets in the pan - not touching. You can prepare in batches or use two sheet pans.
5. Bake the chips on the bottom oven rack (10-15 min.).
6. Meanwhile, crush the salt with the dried chives and sprinkle the beets.
7. Wait for the beets to cool in the pan.
8. Once cooled, scoop them onto a cooling rack to finish drying.

Cranberry - Goat Cheese & Walnut Canapés

Servings Provided: 9

Preparation & Cooking Time: 30 minutes

What You Need

- Baguette - whole wheat (24 thin slices)
- Walnuts (.75 cup - approx. 24 halves)
- Ground pepper & coarse salt
- Ground cinnamon (.125 or 1/8 tsp.)
- Olive oil (4 tsp.)
- Dried cranberries (.5 cup)
- Fresh goat cheese (8 oz./230 g)
- Water (2 tbsp.)
- Fresh chopped thyme (1 tsp + leaves for garnishing)

How To Prepare

1. Set the oven temperature to reach 375° Fahrenheit/191° Celsius.
2. Use a baking sheet with high sides, and add oil (1 tsp.), salt, pepper, and cinnamon. Toss in the nuts to bake (4-6 min.). Scoop them into a holding dish.
3. Using the same sheet, add the baguette slices and brush with oil - flavoring with pepper and salt.
4. Bake for 10 to 15 minutes. Rotate the pan halfway through the cooking process.
5. Now, mix the water with the cheese. Mix in the thyme and cranberries with a dash of pepper or salt.
6. Serve the goat cheese with the slices of bread. Garnish each one with thyme leaves and a few walnuts.

Cucumber Roll-Ups

Servings Provided: 6

Preparation & Cooking Time: 5-10 minutes

What You Need

- Cucumber (1 large)
- Crumbled feta (.6 tbsp.)
- Roasted – chopped red pepper/sun-dried tomatoes (6 tbsp.)
- Roasted garlic hummus (6 tbsp.)
- Black pepper (.125 or 1/8 tsp.)

How To Prepare

1. Slice off long strips of the cucumber using a veggie peeler or knife. Discard the seeds. You should easily get 12 strips. Sprinkle with the pepper.
2. Spread the hummus on each slice and garnish. Roll them up and secure with a toothpick.

Falafel Smash

Servings Provided: 3-4

Preparation & Cooking Time: 15 minutes

What You Need
- Cooked chickpeas (1.5 cups)
- Salt (.25 tsp.)
- Ground cumin & coriander (1 tsp. each)
- Crushed red pepper (.25 tsp.)
- Juiced lemon (half of 1)
- Olive oil (1 tbsp.)
- Plain non-dairy yogurt (.25 cup)
- Pea shoots or arugula (2-3 handfuls)
- Pickled or raw red onion (thin slices) or other pickled veggies (several slices)
- Homemade or store-bought pita bread (4-6)

    The Sauce:
- Garlic (1 clove)
- Cilantro with stems - finely chopped (2 large handfuls)
- Olive oil (.25 cup)
- Toasted sesame seeds (2 tbsp.)
- Salt (Big pinch)

How To Prepare
1. Rinse and drain the beans. Lightly mash the chickpeas with a fork or pulse them in a food processor. Mince/crush the garlic.
2. Stir in the salt, ground coriander, crushed red pepper, ground cumin, lemon juice, and oil.
3. Finely chop the cilantro and toss with the rest of the cilantro sauce fixings.
4. Layer the dish starting with the yogurt, pea shoots/arugula, chickpea mix, cilantro sauce, and pickled/raw red onion on the bread and serve.

Grab & Go Snack Jars

Servings Provided: 4

Preparation & Cooking Time: 15 minutes

What You Need
- Red & yellow bell pepper (1 each)
- Snap pea crisps (1 handful)
- Guacamole (.5 cup)
- Hummus (.5 cup)
- Peanut butter (.5 cup)
- Grape tomatoes (.5 cup)
- Celery (2 stalks)
- Blueberries (.25 cup)
- Strawberries (.5 cup)
- Greek yogurt (.5 cup - plain)
- Granola (.5 cup)
- Pretzels (.5 cup)
- Pint mason jars & tops

How To Prepare
1. Prep the first jar of bell peppers and hummus. Slice peppers into 1/4-inch strips. Add a layer of hummus, and top with sliced peppers. Seal and pop it into the fridge.
2. Add the guacamole and black bean crisps to jar two. Add the guacamole, add in tomatoes, then top with bean habanero crisps. Seal and add it to the refrigerator. (Eat it within one day or they will be mushy.)
3. Prep a parfait jar. First, slice the strawberries. Then scoop in yogurt, granola, strawberries, and blueberries. Close the jar and add it to the collection.
4. Prepare a peanut butter and celery jar by slicing the celery into three-inch slices. Layer peanut butter at the bottom, then celery stick, and top with pretzels. Seal the lid and add it to the other three, but be sure to use it within 24-48 hours, so the pretzels don't get soggy.
5. Grab your snacks anytime. They are excellent for a quick lunch or a trip to the park for the day. Mix them any way desired.

Mediterranean Eggplant Chips

Servings Provided: 4-6

Preparation & Cooking Time: Varies - 5 hours 15 minutes

What You Need

- Baby eggplants (6)
- Olive oil (.25 cup)
- Smoked paprika (1 tsp.)
- Garlic powder (.5 tsp.)
- Cayenne pepper (.25 tsp.)
- Oregano (.5 tsp.)
- Black pepper & kosher salt (to your liking)

How To Prepare

1. Thinly slice (lengthwise) the eggplant into a big mixing container.
2. Whisk the oil with the spices and add to the bowl - gently tossing till the eggplant pieces are coated with the spices.
3. Arrange the slices on the trays of a dehydrator to dehydrate on the fruits/vegetable setting (@ 135° Fahrenheit/57° Celsius – 4-5 hr.) until fully dried and crisp.
4. Be sure to check the trays around three to four hours. Cool thoroughly before storing.

Pita Pizzas & Hummus

Servings Provided: 6-8

Preparation & Cooking Time: 25 minutes

What You Need
- Pita bread (5 slices)
- Beef roast (1 cup)
- Artichokes (.5 cup)
- Whole tomatoes (10 oz./280 g can)
- Chopped olives (.5 cup)
- Olive oil (10 tbsp.)
- Tahini (1 tbsp.)
- Chickpeas (1 cup)
- Garbanzo beans (1 cup)
- Oregano (1 tsp.)
- Lemon (half of 1)
- Feta cheese (.5 cup)
- Paprika and salt (as desired)

How To Prepare
1. Set the oven at 250° Fahrenheit/121° Celsius.
2. Blend the can of tomatoes for the sauce.
3. Split the bread into halves on a baking tin. On each slice, sprinkle a touch of oil along with sauce (1 tbsp.). Next, place the artichokes, roast beef, cheese, and black olives. Top off with the salt and oregano.
4. Place the tray on the broiler five minutes. Let it cool 3-4 minutes.
5. *For the Hummus*: Use a blender to combine 1 tablespoon of the Tahini, 1 tablespoon oil, salt, a pinch of paprika, ½ of a lemon, and 1 cup each of the garbanzo and chickpeas.
6. Serve the hummus along with the pizza as a healthier snack food.
7. *Note*: If the hummus mixture is too dry, just add a little more olive oil.

Smoked Salmon & Avocado Summer Rolls

Servings Provided: 12 rolls

Preparation & Cooking Time: 20 minutes

What You Need

- Rice paper wrappers (12 rounds)
- Avocado (1)
- Smoked salmon (6 slices)
- Raw sprouts or cooked vermicelli (2-3 cups)
- English cucumber (1 seeded - cut into strips)
- For Dipping: Miso sesame dressing or fish sauce vinaigrette

How To Prepare

1. Plunge a rice paper wrapper into a dish of hot tap water (10-15 sec.).
2. Then, put the wrapper on a chopping block.
3. Thinly slice the salmon and avocado. Add fillings the way you like them.
4. Roll them like a burrito.
5. Dip in the miso sesame dressing or fish sauce vinaigrette and serve.

Dips

Feta Dip

Servings Provided: 6

Preparation & Cooking Time: 10 minutes

What You Need
- Feta block (8 oz. or 230 g)
- Fresh parsley & mint (2 tbsp.)
- Greek yogurt (.75 cup)
- Lemon (1 zested)
- Olive oil (2 tbsp. or as needed)
- Aleppo or red pepper flakes (1 tsp. + as desired)

  Optional Toppings:
- Toasted pine nuts (2-3 tbsp.)
- Pistachios (1-2 tbsp.)
- Also Needed: Big food processor - with a blade

How To Prepare
1. Drain the feta in a colander and chop the mint and parsley. Lastly, crush the pistachios.
2. Mix the feta with the yogurt and lemon zest in the processor. Blend - while the processor is in operation with a drizzle of oil through the top opening until the feta is whipped to a smooth mixture.
3. Transfer the mixture onto a serving platter. Smooth the top of the feta, making an indentation/well in the center.
4. Pour a tiny bit of oil over the feta, and top with the Aleppo pepper, fresh herbs, and nuts to serve.

Healthy Basil Pesto

Servings Provided: 16 tablespoons

Preparation & Cooking Time: 10 minutes

What You Need

- Fresh basil leaves (2 cups - packed)
- Garlic cloves (1-2)
- Walnuts/pine nuts - toasted (.33 or 1/3 cup)
- Olive oil (.5 cup + more for storing)
- Grated parmesan cheese - fine (.5 cup)
- Black pepper & kosher salt (as desired)
- Juiced lemon (half of 1)
- Also Needed: Food processor - with a blade

How To Prepare

1. Quickly blanch the basil and put it into a container of ice water on the countertop.
2. Next, fill a saucepan halfway with water and wait for it to boil.
3. Drop the basil leaves in the pan to blanch until wilted (5-10 sec.). Using tongs, scoop the leaves into the ice container to prevent further cooking.
4. Thoroughly dry the leaves by wrapping them in paper towels (gently squeezing).
5. Roughly chop the garlic.
6. Prepare the pesto by adding the basil, pine nuts, garlic, and lemon juice into the food processor. Allow the unit to continue running as you slowly add in the oil.
7. Transfer the basil mixture into a mixing container and fold in the parmesan, pepper, and salt as desired – gently tossing - adding oil as desired.
8. Use immediately or store for later. It is easily stored in a mason jar in the fridge for about seven days. Then, be sure to cover it with a thin layer of oil to prevent air from reaching the sauce.

Spring Pea & Fava Bean Guacamole With Root Chips

Servings Provided: 2-3

Preparation & Cooking Time: 55-60 minutes

What You Need

The Root Chips:

- Olive oil
- Root vegetables (5 large- mix of golden/red beets or turnips)
- Salt (as desired)

The Guacamole:

- Fava beans (5-6 **)
- English peas (20)
- Avocados (4 ripe)
- Juiced lemon (half of 1)
- Cilantro (a handful)
- Red onion (half of 1 small -about 1/4 cup)
- Smoked paprika (1 pinch)
- Black pepper & salt
- Optional: Red pepper flakes (1 dash)

How To Prepare

1. Make the root chips by preheating the oven to 300° Fahrenheit/149° Celsius.
2. Cover a big baking tray with a layer of parchment baking paper.
3. Thinly slice the roots using a mandolin (not paper thin). Layer them onto the prepared baking tray. Lightly brush them with oil (no salt yet).
4. Place another piece of parchment over the roots and then lay another baking sheet on top.
5. Bake the chips (20 min.). Pull them out and remove the baking sheet that is on top and place them back in the oven (15-20 min.). Remove the ones that have browned on the edges.
6. When they're done, transfer the chips to a wire rack to cool and harden. Lastly, dust them as desired with salt.
7. Meanwhile, add water to a pot and wait for it to boil. Also, make a container of ice for an 'ice bath.'

8. Toss the favas and beans into the boiling water to simmer (3-4 min.). When they're tender, remove and add to the ice bath (2 min.). Now, strain the peas and beans as you remove them from the ice bath.
9. Smash the avocado with a fork until it's as desired. Add the lemon juice, chopped cilantro, finely chopped red onion, and smoked paprika and stir to combine. Add the salt, pepper, and red pepper flakes to your liking.
10. Top with the peas and fava beans and serve immediately with the root chips.

*Removing the Beans***

1. First, take the beans from the pods by running a finger up the seam of the pod (4-5 in each pod).
2. Also discard its thick whiteish skin around it. There are two different methods. The first is to make a small slit with a knife along the edge of the bean to pop the bean out of its skin. Or toss the fava beans into a pot of boiling salted water to blanch (1/2 minute). Scoop the beans from the boiling water and immediately plunge them in ice cold water to halt the cooking process. This will make the second skin layer simpler to remove.
3. Squeeze the bean out from its skin by pushing it with your fingers.
4. You now have usable beans for your recipe.

Chapter 11: Mediterranean Dessert Specialties

Fanouropita - Saint Fanourios Cake

Servings Provided: 8 to 10

Preparation & Cooking Time: 60 minutes

What You Need
- Orange juice (1 cup)
- Seed oil – your preference (1 cup)
- Granulated sugar (1 cup)
- Cinnamon (1 tsp.)
- Ground clove (.5 tsp.)
- Baking soda (1 tsp.)
- Self-rising flour (3 cups)
- Walnuts - chopped (80 g/ 3 oz.)
- Raisins (3 oz.)

How To Prepare
1. Set the oven temperature to 340° Fahrenheit/171° Celsius.
2. Add the sugar and vegetable oil to a big mixing container. Using a hand whisk, beat until the sugar dissolves.
3. In another container, combine the orange juice with the baking soda and mix using a fork until the baking soda froths and dissolves completely.
4. Add the orange juice and baking soda mixture to the bowl with the sugar and oil. Whisk thoroughly.
5. In another bowl, add the flour, ground cinnamon, ground clove, raisins, and chopped walnuts. Mix using a wooden spoon.
6. Blend the flour mixture with the liquid mixture, a little bit at a time, while whisking. Mix until the fixings are thoroughly combined, and the mixture is smooth like a thick batter.

7. Transfer the mixture for the fanouropita into a round oiled baking pan 28cm in diameter and bake (45 min. to 1 hr.). To check if the fanouropita is ready, stick a toothpick in the cake. If the toothpick comes out clean, it's ready. If not, bake a little longer and check again.
8. Leave it in the pan to thoroughly cool before removing it from the pan.
9. Serve the fanouropita with icing sugar.

Greek Yogurt Cheesecake

Servings Provided: 10

Preparation & Cooking Time: 12-15 minutes

What You Need
- Golden Oreo cookies – crushed (28)
- Plain – full-fat Greek yogurt (4 cups)
- Sweetened Condensed milk (14 oz./400 g can)
- Optional Topping: Cookies (4)
- Also Needed: 9-inch/23-cm round pie dish

How To Prepare
1. Add the golden cookies to a food processor and work them into crumbs.
2. Scoop the crumbs into the pie dish and press down with the back of a spoon.
3. Add the yogurt and condensed milk to a microwave-safe bowl, thoroughly mixing.
4. Microwave for three minutes - stir well again.
5. Return to the microwave for another three minutes, stir, and dump it over the crumb base - smoothing with the back of a spoon.
6. Place the container in the fridge overnight to set.
7. At serving time, crush four cookies over the top and slice to serve.

Greek Yogurt Parfait With Nuts & Kahlua

Servings Provided: 4

Preparation & Cooking Time: 25 minutes

What You Need

- Fat-free Greek yogurt (3 cups)
- Light - whipped cream (1 cup)
- Sugar (.5 cup)
- Cinnamon (1 tsp.)
- Kahlua rum - divided (4 tbsp.)
- Vanilla extract (1 tsp.)
- Raisins (.5 cup)
- Pistachios (.5 cup)
- Hazelnuts (.5 cup)

How To Prepare

1. Before you begin, shell, and roughly chop the nuts and measure the rest of the fixings.
2. Load a microwave-safe bowl and combine raisins with Kahlua (2 tbsp.). Warm it in the microwave (50 sec.). Stir and return it to cook for another ½ minute. Raisins will have absorbed Kahlua and become nice and plump. Set aside for now.
3. Use a food processor to roughly chop pistachios and hazelnuts.
4. Use a hand mixer to combine the yogurt, whipped cream, sugar, rest of the Kahlua, vanilla extract, and cinnamon.
5. You can cover and refrigerate the yogurt mixture for an hour or until you're ready to put them together.
6. To assemble, add two to three tablespoons of the yogurt mixture into the bottom of your serving glass. Then, add a layer of the nuts and Kahlua raisins.
7. Top with one tablespoon of the yogurt mixture and garnish with a few of the nuts.

Greek Yogurt Pumpkin Parfait

Servings Provided: 6

Preparation & Cooking Time: 5 minutes

What You Need

- Pumpkin puree (15 oz./430 g can or scant 2 cups if homemade)
- Low-fat Greek yogurt (1.25 cups)
- Mascarpone cheese (3 to 4 tbsp.)
- Vanilla extract (1 tsp.)
- Molasses (2 tbsp/ + more to garnish)
- Brown sugar (2.5 tbsp.)
- Cinnamon (1.5 to 2 tsp.)
- Nutmeg (1 dash)

  To Garnish:
- Chocolate chips
- Chopped hazelnuts or walnuts
- *Suggested*: 3-oz./85 g serving goblets/mason jars

How To Prepare

1. Load a mixing container with the Greek yogurt, pumpkin puree, and the rest of the fixings (omit the nuts and chocolate chips). Using a hand electric mixer or a whisk, work the fixings to reach a silky consistency.
2. Taste test it and adjust the flavor to your liking, mixing thoroughly.
3. Transfer the pumpkin-yogurt mixture into serving dishes or jars. Cover and pop it into the fridge for 30 minutes or overnight.
4. At serving time, add a drizzle of molasses, chocolate chips, and chopped nuts.

Honey Pie With Ricotta Cheese

Servings Provided: 8

Preparation & Cooking Time: 1 hour 25 minutes

What You Need

The Pie:

- Ricotta cheese (2.5 cups)
- Honey (.5 cup)
- Sugar (.25 cup)
- Eggs (3)
- Vanilla (1 tbsp.)
- Optional: Pomegranate seeds

The Pan:

- Round or springform pan (8-inch) **
- Cornstarch (1 tsp.)
- Butter (as needed)

How To Prepare

1. Set the oven temperature at 375° Fahrenheit or 191° Celsius.
2. Whisk each of the pie components in a mixing container.
3. Grease the cake pan with butter and sprinkle it using cornstarch.
4. Empty the batter into the pan to bake until it is browned and set in the center (approx. 1 hr.).
5. Cool and then flip the cake from the pan and flip back over onto a serving plate or use a springform pan**.
6. Garnish with more honey and a dusting of cinnamon, and pomegranate seeds to serve.

Italian Apple & Olive Oil Cake

Servings Provided: 12

Prep & Cooking Time: 1 hour - 15 minutes

What You Need
- Gala apples (2 large)
- Orange juice - for soaking
- Gold raisins (.66 or 2/3 cup)
- Flour – all-purpose (3 cups)
- Nutmeg (.5 tsp.)
- Sugar (1 cup)
- Baking powder & soda (1 tsp. of each)
- Cinnamon (.5 tsp.)
- Olive oil (1 cup)
- Large eggs (2)
- Water (as needed)
- Confectioner's sugar - for dusting
- Also Needed: Baking pan (9-inch/23-cm)

How To Prepare
1. Peel and finely chop the apples. Drizzle the apples with just enough orange juice to prevent browning.
2. Measure and add the raisins to warm water to soak (15 min.) and drain well.
3. Sift the baking powder with the cinnamon, baking soda, nutmeg, and flour. Place the container to the side for now.
4. Pour the oil and sugar into the bowl of a stand mixer. Blend the mixture using the low setting for two minutes or until well combined.
5. Blend while running, break in the eggs "*1 at a time*." Continue to mix for two minutes. The mixture should increase in volume; it should be thick - not runny.
6. Combine all of the fixings. Begin by making a hole in the middle of the flour mix. Add the olive and sugar mixture.

7. Remove the apples of any excess juice and drain the raisins that have been soaking. Add them in with the batter, mixing well.
8. Prepare the baking pan with a layer of parchment baking paper. Spoon and smooth the batter into the pan.
9. Bake it at 350° Fahrenheit or 177° Celsius (45 min.).
10. When ready, carefully transfer the cake from the parchment paper. Put it on a serving platter. Dust it using the confectioner's sugar. Heat the dark honey to garnish the top.

Mango-Peach & Nectarine & Crumble

Servings Provided: 6

Preparation & Cooking Time: 45 minutes

What You Need
- Nectarines (4)
- Mango (half of 1)
- Peaches (2)
- Beet or brown sugar (.25 cup or 50 g)
- Flour (1 cup or 100 g)
- Salted butter (1 cup or 100 g)
- Biscoff cookies or another favorite (8 or 100 g)

How To Prepare
1. Preheat the oven to reach about 350° Fahrenheit/177° Celsius.
2. Cut the fruit into small squares and toss it into in a medium baking dish.
3. Crush the cookies and mix with the flour and sugar. Lastly, mix it with the butter till it's crumbly.
4. Top the fruit with the crumble. Bake for ½ hour until it's as desired.

Mediterranean Chocolate Cake

Servings Provided: 15

Preparation & Cooking Time: 40 to 45 minutes

What You Need

- A. P. flour (2.5 cups)
- Lukewarm water (2 cups)
- Sugar (2 cups)
- Baking powder (3 tsp. - leveled)
- Cocoa powder (1.5 cups)
- Salt (1 pinch)
- Vanilla extract (.5 tsp.)
- Orange (1 zested)

    The Sauce:

- Dark chocolate (7 oz. or 200g)
- Milk (1 oz. or 30ml)
- Butter (1 tbsp.)
- Pan or Dish Needed: 9 x 12-inch or 22×30-cm

How To Prepare

1. Set the oven temperature to reach 338° Fahrenheit or 170° Celsius.
2. Toss the chocolate cake fixings into a big mixing container (flour, cocoa powder, baking powder, sugar, and salt). Thoroughly whisk.
3. Now, using the same bowl, add the water, vanilla essence, and orange zest, whisking it into a cake batter.
4. Butter the baking dish and pour in the cake batter to bake (30 min.).
5. Remove the cake form the oven and wait for it to cool (1-2 hr.).
6. Prepare the sauce in a double boiler. Add the chocolate (small chunks) with the milk and butter - stirring until the chocolate melts and all of the ingredients are incorporated.
7. Use a fork to poke a few holes on the top of the cake and drizzle the sauce over the top.
8. Serve while still warm with a serving of vanilla ice cream.

Middle Eastern Rice Pudding

Servings Provided: 4-6

Preparation & Cooking Time: 50 minutes

What You Need

- 2% milk (2 cups)
- Heavy cream/Half "&" Half (1 cup)
- Vanilla extract (2 tsp.)
- Cinnamon sticks (2)
- Whole cloves (6)
- Medium-grain rice (1 cup)
- Sugar (3 tbsp.)
- Water (.5 cup + more as needed)
- Evaporated milk (.33 or 1/3 cup)
- Unsalted room temp butter (2 tbsp.)
    For Serving:
- Ground cinnamon
- Honey
- Crushed pistachios & walnuts

How To Prepare

1. Measure and add the milk, heavy cream, vanilla extract, cloves, and cinnamon sticks into a saucepan. Use the high-temperature setting to heat the mixture, removing it from the burner right before it starts to boil.
2. Cool thoroughly and refrigerate for a couple of hours to overnight.
3. Take the milk mixture from the fridge and wait for it to become room temp. Add the rice, water, and sugar. Boil it using high heat and simmer – stirring frequently (30-40 min.). If needed, add a little water (2 tbsp. or so at a time).
4. Transfer the pan to the countertop and mix in the evaporated milk and butter.
5. Discard the cloves and sticks of cinnamon and add it to mason jars or another serving dish.
6. When ready to serve, add a little milk if desired and warm it in the microwave, Garnish the dessert with a dash of cinnamon, honey, and nuts to serve.

Raspberry Clafoutis

Servings Provided: 6

Preparation & Cooking Time: 50 minutes

What You Need

- For the Dish: Unsalted butter
- Raspberries (3 cups - 350 g)
- Granulated sugar - divided (.5 cup + 1 tbsp.)
- Optional: Dried lavender buds (1 tsp.)
- Whole milk (.5 cup) whole milk
- Optional: Crème Fraiche (.5 cup/114 g + more to serve)
- Eggs (4 large)
- Salt (1 dash)
- All-purpose flour ⅓ cup (.33 or 1/3 cup or 43 g)
- To Serve: Confectioner's sugar
- Optional: Greek yogurt
- Your Choice Baking Pan: 2-quart gratin dish/9-inch ceramic baking dish/9-inch cake pan

How To Prepare

1. Heat the oven to 375° Fahrenheit/191° Celsius. Butter the baking pan.
2. Toss the raspberries with sugar (1 tbsp.) to marinate.
3. Load a food processor/blender to mix the remainder of the sugar (.5 cup) with the lavender - process until the lavender is mostly ground (2 min.).
4. Then pour the milk, crème Fraiche, eggs, and salt, and process to combine. Mix in the flour - pulsing just to combine.
5. Arrange the sugared berries in the prepared baking dish, then pour the egg mixture over them. Bake until the cake is golden and the center springs back when lightly touched (35 min.).
6. Place the baking dish onto a wire rack and let the cake cool for a minimum of 15 minutes before serving.
7. Sprinkle it with confectioners' sugar, slice it, and serve it with a dollop of whipped crème fraiche if you like.

Sweet Ricotta & Strawberry Parfaits

Servings Provided: 6

Preparation & Cooking Time: 15 minutes (+) chilling time

What You Need

- Fresh strawberries (1 lb./450 g)
- Snipped fresh mint (1 tbsp.)
- Sugar (1 tsp.)
- Part-skim ricotta cheese (15 oz./430 g carton)
- Light agave nectar (3 tbsp.)
- Finely shredded lemon peel (.25 tsp.)
- Vanilla (.5 tsp.)
- The Topping: Fresh mint

How To Prepare

1. Mix the berries with the sugar and mint in a mixing bowl. Gently stir. Let it rest about ten minutes.
2. In another container, mix the agave nectar, ricotta, lemon peel, and vanilla. Combine it using an electric mixer (2 min. @ medium speed).
3. Prepare the parfaits. Scoop one tablespoon of the mixture into each of the glasses. Top it off with the strawberry combination. Repeat the layers and garnish with the mint.
4. Serve right away or cover and chill for up to four hours.

Tahini Brownies

Servings Provided: 16

Preparation & Cooking Time: 38-40 minutes

What You Need

- Salted butter (4 tbsp. + as needed for the skillet)
- Dark – bittersweet chocolate chips (4 oz. or 110 g)
- Cocoa powder (3 tbsp.)
- Eggs (2 large)
- White sugar (1 cup + 2 tbsp.)
- Kosher salt (1 tsp.)
- Tahini (.75 cup)
- Vanilla extract (1 tbsp.)
- Flour – all-purpose is okay (.33 or 1/3 cup)
- Also Needed: 8-inch or 20-cm square pan + tin foil

How To Prepare

1. Heat the oven to reach 350° Fahrenheit/177° Celsius.
2. Cover the baking pan with two pieces of foil (crossed with excess hanging over the pan's sides). Lightly brush the foil with a little butter.
3. Now warm a saucepan using a medium temperature to melt the butter. Remove the pan from the burner and mix in the cocoa and chocolate chips – whisking till it's silky.
4. Whisk the eggs with the vanilla, salt, and sugar till slightly thickened. Now, mix in the tahini. Mix in the flour. Reserve half of the tahini mixture.
5. Add the melted chocolate mixture to the rest of the tahini mixture, stirring till it's thoroughly mixed. Empty and evenly spread the batter into the pan.
6. With a spoon, dollop the reserved tahini mixture over the top. Swirl the tahini dollops into the batter.
7. Put the pan on the centermost rack of the heated oven.
8. Bake till the edges are set but the center remains moist (28-30 min.).
9. Transfer the pan to the countertop to cool (½ hr.)
10. Carefully lift the foil edges to transfer the brownies from the pan.
11. Cool for another ½ hour but don't remove from the foil yet. Slice them into two-inch squares, then serve or store when thoroughly cooled.

Chapter 12: Mediterranean 30-Day Kick-Start Meal Plan

Please enjoy the selections provided using your new recipes!

Week One Kick-Off

Day of the Week	Breakfast	Lunch	Dinner	Snack or Dessert
Day 1	Avocado & Egg Breakfast Sandwich	Egg & Lemon Greek Soup	Pan Seared Mahi-Mahi	Saint Fanourios Cake
Day 2	Blackberry-Ginger Overnight Bulgur	Black Olive & Feta Turkey Burgers	Beef Steaks Crusted in Cumin with Olive-Orange Relish	Middle Eastern Rice Pudding
Day 3	Avocado & Egg Breakfast Sandwich	Chickpea Salad	Pork Tenderloin & Couscous	Leftover Saint Fanourios Cake
Day 4	Breakfast Quinoa	Homemade Vegetable Soup	Seared Tuna Steaks	Greek Yogurt Parfait with Nuts & Kahlua
Day 5	Frisco Fried Egg & Cheese Breakfast	Cannellini Pasta	Grilled Lamb Chops & Mint	Date & Prosciutto Wraps

Day 6	Greek Peanut Butter & Banana Yogurt Bowl	Sweet & Spicy Jicama Salad	Braised Chicken with the Trimmings	Honey-Almond Peaches
Day 7	Greek Egg Frittata	Vegetarian Lasagna Roll-Ups	Lebanese Grilled Shish Tawook	Leftover Date & Prosciutto Wraps

Week Two Mediterranean Plan

Day of the Week	Breakfast	Lunch	Dinner	Snack or Dessert
Day 8	Nutty Banana Oatmeal	Lentil Greek Soup	Moroccan Fish Favorite	Greek Yogurt Cheesecake
Day 9	Greek Quinoa Breakfast Bowl	Tuna Antipasto Salad	Grilled Beef Lettuce Wraps With Garlic-Yogurt Sauce	Delicious Energy Bites
Day 10	Pumpkin Pancakes	Chicken-Feta Burgers	Rosemary Pork Loin Chops	Leftover Greek Yogurt Cheesecake
Day 11	Shakshuka Skillet Dish	Greek Tabbouleh Salad	Frozen Italian Fish	Mango-Peach & Nectarine & Crumble
Day 12	Tahini Date Banana Shake	Meatball Soup	Roasted Leg of Lamb with Potatoes	Honey Pie with Ricotta Cheese
Day 13	Turkish Poached Eggs in Garlicky Yogurt Sauce	Rigatoni with Asiago Cheese & Green Olive-Almond Pesto	Chicken Marrakesh	Leftover Delicious Energy Bites
Day 14	Whole Grain Citrus & Olive Oil Muffins	Garden Wrap	Beef Kofta + Greek Green Beans	Leftover Honey Pie with Ricotta Cheese

Week Three Mediterranean Plan

Day of the Week	Breakfast	Lunch	Dinner	Snack or Dessert
Day 15	Breakfast Couscous	Chicken Gyros with Tzatziki Sauce	Herbed Salmon	Italian Apple & Olive Oil Cake
Day 16	Honey & Fig Yogurt	Mediterranean Stew	Beef & Couscous Favorite	Honey-Almond Peaches
Day 17	4-Cheese Zucchini Strata	Shrimp & Angel Hair Pasta	Grape & Grilled Chicken Skewers	Leftover Italian Apple & Olive Oil Cake
Day 18	Blueberry Muffins	Lebanese Lentil Salad	Roasted Balsamic Pork Loin	Sweet Ricotta & Strawberry Parfaits
Day 19	Goat Cheese Frittata & Kale	Mediterranean Lamb Nachos	Pan-Seared Sea Bass	Popped Quinoa Crunch Bars
Day 20	Leftover Blueberry Muffins	Parmesan Soup - Gluten-Free	Lemon Thyme Chicken with Fingerlings	Baked Apricots
Day 21	Ham & Egg Cups	Tuna Spinach Salad	Stuffed Eggplant + Broccoli Pasta with White Beans	Leftover Popped Quinoa Crunch Bars

Week Four Mediterranean Plan

Day of the Week	Breakfast	Lunch	Dinner	Snack or Dessert
Day 22	Greek Honey & Walnut Yogurt Bowl	Mediterranean Lamb Bowls	Pan-Seared Salmon & Asparagus	Mediterranean Chocolate Cake
Day 23	Mediterranean Eggs on Toast	Beef Pitas	Chicken Souvlaki	Honey Pistachio Roasted Pears
Day 24	Blackberry-Ginger Overnight Bulgur	Persian Chilled Cucumber Soup	Balsamic Lamb Chops	Leftover Mediterranean Chocolate Cake
Day 25	Spinach Omelet	Honey-Walnut Salad with Feta & Raisins	Roasted Cod With Olive-Tomato-Caper Tapenade	Raspberry Clafoutis
Day 26	Breakfast Quinoa	Lamb Lettuce Wraps	Honey Lemon Pork Chops	Greek Honey Sesame Bars
Day 27	Avocado & Egg Breakfast Sandwich	Greek Yogurt with Cucumber & Dill Salad	Lemon-Za'atar - Grilled Chicken	Easy Roasted Fruit
Day 28	Pumpkin Pancakes	White Bean Chili	Loaded Portobello Burger	Tahini Brownies

Week Five Mediterranean Plan

Day of the Week	Breakfast	Lunch	Dinner	Snack or Dessert
Day 29	Greek Egg Frittata	Delightful Quinoa Salad	Lemony Chicken Skewers	Leftover Greek Honey Sesame Bars
Day 30	Whole Grain Citrus & Olive Oil Muffins	Fruit Salad with Honey-Mint Sauce	Lamb Chops with Rosemary & Thyme	Leftover Tahini Brownies

Now you have the plan, get started on your new way of eating. Please Enjoy!

If you enjoyed this book, please let me know your thoughts by leaving a short review on Amazon! Thank you so much!

Get my future books for FREE!!
Check this page: https://mirandasharron.aweb.page/p/77acd671-2d38-45e7-92c7-ef7e9d41ba64

Printed in Great Britain
by Amazon